INSIDE THE

HOUSE *of* LORDS

HarperCollins*Publishers*

General Sir Edward Jones, KCB, CBE, Gentleman Usher of the Black Rod, in the Peers' Lobby.
The doors behind him give into the Chamber of the House of Lords

INSIDE THE
HOUSE
of LORDS

CLIVE ASLET & DERRY MOORE

First published in 1998 by
HarperCollins*Publishers*, London

Text © Clive Aslet 1998
Commissioned photographs © Derry Moore 1998

Designer: Willie Landels
Copy Editor: Carole McGlynn
Indexer: Ian Crane

A CIP catalogue record for this book is available from the
British Library.

ISBN 000 414 047 8

Colour origination by Colourscan, Singapore
Printed and bound in Italy by L.E.G.O. SpA

PAGE 3: *The mace*

PAGES 6-7: *View of the Houses of Parliament from the South Bank,*
with Westminster Abbey in the background

Contents

Key escutcheon and handle on a drawer designed by Pugin, showing the care lavished on every detail of the House of Lords

PREFACE

Three years ago, I interviewed Tony Blair, then Leader of the Opposition, and asked him about the Labour Party's recently declared policy to reform the House of Lords. Apparently he sensed that the editor of *Country Life* might approach the question from a pre-established position. 'You must be its house magazine,' he joked. That, perhaps, was doing *Country Life* rather too much honour, though it reflects the general truth that some of the subjects – good subjects, too – on which the Lords is expert (the countryside, wildlife, historic architecture) find a natural forum in its pages. I was not wholly ignorant of the Lords when I began writing this book, but I soon found that the extent of my knowledge was far less than it might have been. Most people, I suspect, are like my former self in having only a hazy impression of the British Upper House. But it befits everyone in a democracy to take an interest in the constitutional arrangements by which their lives are governed and, in this book, I attempt to describe what the House of Lords is today.

This could not be done without investigating the peers that compose the Lords. To that end I have been meeting many of them: of all political parties, all ages, all types of creation (hereditary peers, life peers, law lords, bishops), each with a different point of view on the question of reform. It has been a fascinating experience. Quite apart from the relevance to this book, the interviews provided a profound and extraordinary study in human individuality. I enjoyed every moment of my research. That is in part because of the environment in which it generally took place: Barry and Pugin's building is one of the great masterpieces of European architecture. I have concentrated as much on the history of the building as that of the parliamentary assembly itself, since there are few institutions through the world whose character is as much shaped by its surroundings. A House of Lords that met in a different building would not be the House of Lords that exists today.

None of this explains the genesis of the book. The idea was Derry Moore's: as Earl of Drogheda he has known the building intimately for a long time and two years ago set about photographing it. This grew into a project to record not just the architecture (which, we hope, will remain the same) but also the people and the activities associated with it (which may well change), on the eve of Mr Blair's promised reform.

There are many people whom Derry and I must thank for help with this book. The project would not have been possible at all without the assistance of Black Rod, who literally caused all doors to be opened. Both he and the Clerk of the Parliaments, Michael Davies, did what they could to prevent the author from stumbling into error: any mistake that does occur in the text is entirely of his own making. We are specially grateful to Lady Sandra Wedgwood for guidance on everything concerning the architectural history.

In addition, we must thank all the peers and others who have been so generous to us with their time (in the case of interviews) and patience (in the case of photography). We are proud to say that no one refused us. The galaxy of those people who have helped us is so full of stars that it would be difficult to list them all comprehensively. Those to whom we owe a particular debt include:

The Lord Bishop of London; The Lord Ampthill; The Lord Beloff; The Lord Callaghan of Cardiff; The Lord Campbell of Croy; The Lord Carrington; The Lord Carter; Major Michael Charlesworth, Staff Superintendent; The Marquess of Cholmondeley; Viscount Cranborne; The Baroness Dunn; The Earl Ferrers; The Lord Freyberg; The Lord Goff of Chieveley; The Lord Halsbury; The Lord Hattersley; Air Vice Marshall David Hawkins, Yeoman Usher of the Black Rod; Malcolm Hay; Peter Llewelyn Gwynn-Jones, The Garter Principal King of Arms; The Lord Healey; The Lord Hurd of Westwell; The Lady Hylton-Foster; The Lord Chancellor, Lord Irvine of Lairg; The Lord Jakobovits; The Baroness James; The Baroness Jay; The Lord Jenkin of Roding; The Lord Jenkins of Hillhead; David Johnson; General Sir Edward Jones, Gentleman Usher of the Black Rod; The Earl of Lindsay; The Lord Lloyd-Webber; The Lord Lucas of Chilworth; The Lord McKay of Clashfern; The Baroness Mallalieu; The Lord Mancroft; The Lord Marlesford; The Lord Nolan; The Lord Peston; The Lord Puttnam; The Lord Renton; The Lord Richard; Pollyanne Roberts; Professor The Earl Russell; The Earl of Selborne; Michael Skelton, Principal Doorkeeper, House of Lords and all the doorkeepers; The Baroness Strange; The Lord Strabolgi; Nicholas True; The Baroness Trumpington; The Lord Weatherill; Sir Michael Wheeler-Booth; The Lord Wilberforce; The Lord Williams of Elvel and all the staff at the House of Lords Information Office.

CORINTHIAN CAPITAL OR INTOLERABLE NUISANCE?

'Nobility is a graceful ornament to the civil order.
It is the Corinthian capital of polished society.'
EDMUND BURKE, *Reflections on the Revolution in France*, 1790

'Deluded, bamboozled Englishmen have already discovered that the noble class is an
intolerable nuisance, incompatible with the public good.'
What ought to be done with the things called 'Lords'?
Pamphlet at the time of the Great Reform Bill

The House of Lords is, almost literally, an incredible institution. You can hardly believe it. Nobody would have invented it, in its present form. Nobody *could* have done so: no single brain, even that of a constitutional genius or comic-opera librettist, could have devised the peculiar means of selection, the character of those attending, the rigmarole to which grown men happily (usually it is happily) submit themselves, the anomalies, the curiosity of the traditions or the panoply of the architecture (it took both Charles Barry and Augustus Pugin to do that). Nor, in an age of democracy, can very much of it be defended, except by one cogent argument – the most cogent of all: most people, certainly if they are peers, seem to think that it works. Governments wishing to reform Britain's Upper House are apt to find it a tough bird to chew.

The Lords has influence, but remarkably little power: that lies in the Commons. But it is the senior house. Its history is longer; constitutionally, the Commons looks up to the Lords just as it looks up to the monarch. Its Chamber rather than that of the Commons, is, strictly speaking, the Parliament, for it is only there that the three estates of the realm – Monarch, Lords and Commons – assemble together (albeit, these days, only at the State Opening of Parliament). This hierarchy is expressed in the architecture. The Palace of Westminster is still exactly that – a royal palace – and the most ornate, most gilded parts are those associated with the Queen. Decoratively, the climax of the whole work is the Queen's throne in the Lords' Chamber. Naturally, since the monarch has not been *persona grata* in the Commons since the Civil War, these areas of pageantry occur only on the Lords' side of the building. And the whole of the Lords, being the Upper House, is more sumptuous than the Commons. There is more carving, more colour and more gold. The architecture of the Commons implies that, to its nineteenth-century creators, it might just as well have been peopled with tradesmen as Members of Parliament. It is the Lords that forms, as *The Illustrated London News* ineffably put it on April 17, 1847, 'the most elaborate specimen – the artistical nucleus, as it were, of the superb and stupendous whole'.

In the twentieth century these differences have been exaggerated by the Blitz – a time still remembered by the 90-year-old Lady Hylton-Foster, until two years ago the convenor of the unaffiliated cross-bench peers in the House of Lords. It was then her nightly job, as a Red Cross nurse whose father happened to be the Speaker of the House of Commons, to patrol the dozen or so first-aid posts around the blackened corridors of the Palace with the aid of nothing but a pencil torch. ('One night I got lost,' she remembers. 'I sat down on something and found it was the woolsack.') Bombing destroyed Barry and Pugin's Commons Chamber and blew out most of Pugin's glass from the palace, but it did little damage to the Lords. When the Commons was rebuilt after the war, its decoration was simplified, while that in the Lords survived with every crocket and trefoil of its original splendour. The architectural richness of the Lords was the original inspiration for this book and for Derry Moore's photographs. We have also sought to make a record of the place on the eve of what could be a seismic reform.

Evening view of the Houses of Parliament, seen from Westminster Bridge. A party can be glimpsed taking place on the terrace

The woolsack, upon which the Lord Chancellor sits when he is present in the Chamber, originally symbolized the supremacy of England's trade in wool

THE PEERS

The best moment to see the Lords is at Question Time, which starts each day's afternoon business. Go in person, and your first impression is probably of the Chamber itself: rich, solemn, encrusted with decoration and dominated at one end by the blaze of gold which is the throne – on all occasions except the State Opening of Parliament, an empty seat. Red is the colour: it has been since the sixteenth century. Look a little more closely, and you will start to think that the architecture is telling you something. There are knights in the canopy above the throne, knightly figures (in fact Magna Carta barons) along the walls between the windows, frescoes – when you look for them – showing the Black Prince and other chivalric heroes, and all manner of heraldic devices in the ceiling, if only distance and the bright lights necessary for the television cameras would let you see them. The theme of valour is interwoven with that of religion, since much of the ornament, with its angels and other carvings, might have come from a church. A large fresco above the throne depicts the Baptism of King Ethelbert by St Augustine. As represented through the decoration, this is an Upper House for saints and heroes.

But then regard the peers, sitting on their leather benches in rows, rather as though they were in a particularly well-appointed railway carriage. They are obviously not saints or heroes as pictured by the Victorians. But they are there, in quantity. Television can give the impression that the chamber is poorly attended and certainly it is not always full. But at Question Time, perhaps unexpectedly, every seat on the benches may be taken. Peers who cannot fit on to the benches will have lodged themselves on any available surface. Some stand at the bar: so to speak, the altar rail that separates the holy of holies from the outside world. In the middle of the room, in front of the throne, reposes the rather lonely figure of the Lord Chancellor, isolated both by his position on the woolsack and the unusual circumstance of his wearing a long grey wig. The three clerks behind their table also wear gowns and wigs: short wigs but of different styles, either soft and round like a powder puff or rolled into hard curls. Between the Lord Chancellor and the clerks, more peers – some distinguished ones, too – perch on banquettes (these banquettes are in fact subsidiary woolsacks). It gives the proceedings, for all the grandeur of the surroundings, a pleasantly informal air.

Peers speak; ministers answer; most of the figures on the benches sit immobile as effigies. But there is a constant current of movement, as the chief whip passes a note to one of the clerks and a doorkeeper, immensely grand in his tail-coat, white tie and gilt chain – far better turned out than any of the peers – scans the faces of those present to deliver a message. They are courteous: my goodness, are they courteous. The courtesy is laid on thick. But this is not, as it may seem to visitors, a theatrical performance, but a working assembly of people who want to get on with the job. A keen eye will see that the bench-ends, with their vigorously carved heraldic beasts, have sustained the occasional knock. The carving is of museum quality, but – to the despair of the scholars associated with its care – this is not a museum. At the end of each reply, a handful of peers half-rise to their feet, then subside again, deferring with good-humoured, if sometimes over-elaborate, grace to the one of their number upon whom it falls to ask the next question. The constant bustle suggests a station waiting room when the train is about to move off.

Ignore all the movement, and even the questions, and run your eyes along those robustly upholstered benches. They present a remarkable study in physiognomy. The rich panelling, with its endlessly repeating linenfold, could almost have been designed for the display of heads. There are heads of all kinds: some familiar from political stardom and media appearances, some unknown outside the Chamber, some intellectual, some etiolated, some fleshly, some shrunken, some bearded with a profusion one had thought to have gone out of fashion with the daguerreotype, some of a singularity so marked as to be almost unbelievable at first sight.

The character and variety of these heads is really one of the wonders of Britain. They show individuality. Often they bear the impress of years, and are none the worse for it. These are not the septuagenarian baby faces that one sees, for example, in the United States, from whose tanned surface all evidence of past struggles has been erased; the physiognomy of Britain's peers is, on the whole, an essay in long experience. Here we have what might be described as a whole menagerie of facial types, from marmoset to marsupial, from ox to osprey, from collie dog to camel. There are peers who are squirrels, peers who are reptiles, peers who are tufted owls. A menagerie or an aquarium: the gene pool from which they are fished is, quite obviously, deep indeed.

THE COMPOSITION OF THE LORDS

Some peers inherit their titles and some are appointed officially by the Queen, but in effect by the Prime Minister of the day, for life. It is for God, rather than man, to say whether this assembly possesses wisdom, but it certainly forms a repository of specialist knowledge. 'I dare say that there is more expertise per square foot here than in any forum in the world,' says the rabbinical scholar Lord Jakobovits. He finds that he must put more effort into preparing a speech for the Lords than for a learned society. Baroness Thatcher, who never seemed to have much time for the Lords when she was Prime Minister, now says there is 'better talent here, particularly in the sciences,' than in the House of Commons. The talent takes various forms, balancing knowledge of the world of politics and men with expertise in science, foreign affairs, agriculture, the arts, justice and religion, which can in turn be broken down into a thousand specialisms from pesticides to fine art auctioneering.

Constitutionally, the role of the House of Lords might be described as follows. It is intended primarily to serve as a check on the House of Commons. It revises legislation but it also sometimes initiates it. It acts as the highest court in the land and the supreme court of appeal. It is a forum in which issues concerning the public are debated. But the formidable concentration of expertise that the Lords represents gives it a dynamic beyond its formal role. Baroness Mallalieu puts it simply: 'It is the ultimate fixing place. Everyone has influence. You can get things done if you care about the subject.' It happens simply by meeting people – the right people. Not that every peer is of equal value in this respect. A sardonic eye is cast over the composition of the House by the hereditary peer Lord Mancroft: 'Some duds are booted upstairs to get them out of the House of Commons or out of the trades union movement, or to free a safe seat for the Government.' One might have said that the duds merge into the wallpaper, if that wallpaper did not happen to be by Pugin, thus hardly suitable camouflage for a grey individual. Certainly, though, they are less conspicuous than the big hitters.

There is no obligation on peers to attend and in this respect, as in others, the arrangements governing the Upper House seem beguilingly ad hoc. Some peers attend all the time, others hardly ever, many as and when their other commitments allow them to. Generally, those who do not intend to make much of a contribution to the Lords do not come. Recently the tally of attendance has been running at over 400 a day, their numbers boosted by the many newly created Labour life peers and those hereditary peers who, cynics say, want to prove their value in order to secure life peerages after reform.

ANOMALOUS, BUT STILL WITH US

'Presumably it is no worse to be appointed by God than by Harold Wilson,' one hereditary peer is remembered as saying. These days, this is not a view to which everyone subscribes. In 1997, the Labour Government came to power with a manifesto commitment to abolish the voting rights of those peers who find themselves in possession of that privilege only by virtue of birth. Since this reform threatens to deconstruct the institution which we know as the House of Lords, it is worth giving some thought to it at the beginning of this book. Probably the last hereditary chamber elsewhere in Western Europe was the relatively short-lived example created with the Restoration of Louis XVIII and Charles X in France, after Napoleon. Even the preamble of our own Parliament Act of 1911, which limited the powers of the Lords to delaying Commons legislation, as opposed to rejecting it outright, states that the hereditaries have been allowed to survive only as a temporary measure, until it could be decided what system of election should take their place.

Perhaps some die-hards among the hereditary peers would make a case for the hereditary principle as a principle: but very few. Most of the hereditaries themselves accept that, on the eve of the twenty-first century, they are an anomaly. They are not representative of democracy; therefore their position cannot be defended. But two questions need to be asked. First, how would this reform, by itself, make the House operate better? Once the functions of the House have been described, most readers will, I suspect, answer: in no way at all. Second, how would it make the Lords more democratic? The response to that is more obvious. Appointment by the prime minister is no more defensible, democratically, than accident of birth. In some ways, less so. It would concentrate even more power in the hands of one individual, or whatever committee he appointed as his agent, reinforcing the recent tendency towards over-mighty central government, which many commentators would like to see reversed. The best that could be hoped of a solely appointed House would be a meritocracy. (At present there are some life peers who exude a suspicion of plutocracy.) It would have nothing to do with democracy.

Even some of the new stars of meritocracy, such as the composer Andrew Lloyd-Webber, see virtue in the old system. Lord Lloyd-Webber is loud in his defence of the hereditaries, saying that they are the ones who do the work. Life peers who are still busy in their careers, such as himself, do not have much time to attend. So he would rather see the abolition of all the life peers, leaving the hereditaries, than the other way round.

This criticism of the system would not be affected by the creation of an appointments committee, as has been mooted, to replace the fiat of the prime minister. Who would appoint the appointers? Peers would become even more beholden to those who created them if, as another suggestion has it, they were appointed for renewable terms. The nation's mind would be eased if appointments were subject to independent public scrutiny, but how could this be achieved? It is inconceivable that the merits of, say, the architect Richard Rogers, recently ennobled, as compared to those of Sir Norman Foster, should be publicly debated, to find which would make the more suitable peer. If reason alone were the judge, which it could never be, the bishops would be pushed off their benches, along with the hereditaries. Unpick one strand and the whole jumper will start to unravel. To quote the Labour magnifico Lord Healey (otherwise an advocate of reform): 'Trying to change it into something rational in the Aristotelian sense would be a dreadful waste of time.'

THE PEOPLE'S PEERS?

One does not have to look at the House of Lords for very long before realizing that the hereditary element is sometimes more representative of the people as a whole than the life peers. More representative, perhaps, than government ministers. For they are outside the political caste. They are not driven in ministerial limousines, surrounded only by people who want to get something out of them, or locked up, like bluebottles, in the political hothouse. They are the only people in Parliament who owe nothing to anyone for their appointment or their place. They are not all of the same personality type. 'They include the disabled and the unemployed,' says Baroness Mallalieu (generously, since she is a Labour working peer who supports reform). 'Among them are the sort of people who could never stand for election. Not necessarily successful in careers.' Even the Labour peer Lord Peston, who feels 'very bitter' about the hereditary element, concedes that the 'only ordinary folk here are the hereditaries'.

These days, relatively few peers own great estates, or have got through life without applying themselves to an occupation. They have careers of all kinds. The third Baron Colwyn, who happens to be chairman of the Lords refreshment committee, is a dentist. He also leads a dance band by night: an activity that causes some clicking of tongues in the dining room among peers who believe in the principle of *le patron mange ici*. Under his entry for Career in Dod's *Parliamentary Companion*, the fifth Baron Monkswell, who takes the Labour whip, puts: 'Has been a van driver and turret lathe setter/operator; Product Quality Engineer, Massey-Ferguson 1972-84; Service Administration Manager 1984-89'. As a trained electrician he joins the gangs of workmen maintaining the Palace of Westminster during the summer recess. Another Labour hereditary, Lord Rea, is a general practitioner – the only one in the House. The seventh Earl of Munster may confirm the public in its stereotyped idea of a Lord by listing field sports among his recreations in *Who's Who*, but, less predictably, he is also an expert on the restoration of stained glass, who has worked for four years as a conservator at the Burrell Collection. The third Earl Attlee, an expert on transport, has been serving with the British Forces in Bosnia.

The twelfth Earl of Drogheda, as readers will realize from this book, is a photographer. Photography is an essential part of daily life, highly controversial in some aspects (think of Princess Diana's death), and yet no prime minister has thought to appoint a photographer as a life peer. There may be a few hereditary peers who are drug addicts (reformed or otherwise) and criminals, but that only illustrates the extent to which, through the almost arbitrary process of selection that is the hereditary system, they reflect the population as a whole. 'The great advantage of the hereditary system is that you are bringing a bit of the unknown into it,' comments Lord Ferrers, a veteran of every Conservative administration since Macmillan. 'The House of Lords has existed for 600 years and has, rightly or wrongly, been based on the hereditary system. You should not discard 600 years of tradition lightly. Why should people like me sit in the House of Lords?' he continues, from his bed in the King Edward VII's Hospital for Officers. 'Well, why should people like me be six foot six and fall and break their hips? That is the way the cards of life are dealt.'

The hereditary peers provide continuity: at 80, Lord Haig has been attending the House for 58 years. More surprisingly, they also provide youth. For all Tony Blair's wish to make Britain a 'young country again', the great and the good whom he has made peers are in middle age (and that, in some cases, is to flatter them). But then a prime qualification for becoming one of the great and the good is experience, which is a function of time. Captains of industry, former ambassadors and governors of Hong Kong, cabinet ministers who have finished their Commons careers, heads of institutions: such people could hardly be in the first flush of youth. So the life peers are, collectively, older than the hereditaries, their average age being 69 while that of the hereditaries is 62. The youngest peers – the ones in their twenties – are all hereditaries. When a peer arrives in the Lords, it takes a certain time to learn the ropes and hereditaries have the advantage of knowing, from an early age, what is in store for them. As a result, they can make their mark felt more quickly.

Some of the hereditary peers who formed part of Conservative administrations in the 1990s were, in political terms, striplings when they became ministers. Lord Strathclyde was 28 when he became House of Lords spokesman for the Department of Trade and Industry. Lord Henley became a government whip – or, more picturesquely, a Lord in waiting: the position in the royal household to which whips are

EARL FERRERS

Lord Ferrers is the beau ideal of a certain type of Englishman. Six foot six inches (2 metres) tall, with penetrating eyes above a white moustache, he looks as immaculately turned out in country tweeds as in his blue House of Lords suit. Having spoken to him in hospital, where he was recovering from a hip operation, I can reveal that the sartorial perfection extends even to his pyjamas. At 69 years old, he is everything you would expect of Winchester, Cambridge and the Coldstream Guards.

In the House of Lords, Lord Ferrers has served every Conservative prime minister since Harold Macmillan – five of them, he says with some pride, without ever having been sacked. 'I think that they forgot I was there.' It is an extraordinary record, though marginally less remarkable in the Lords than it would be in the Commons. In the Lords, ministers tend to stay in place longer. Recalling his spell at the Home Office, from 1988 to 1994, he says: 'I was there for six years, and served under five Home Secretaries and three permanent secretaries. Therefore in a way one was a sort of constant factor.' Alec Douglas-Home, Ted Heath, Margaret Thatcher, John Major – they all came and went, too. Lord Ferrers views it all as 'enormously interesting and a huge privilege,' but warns that 'nobody should think there is a career' in the House of Lords. 'There isn't. You are told what to do and get on with it.'

His first government job, in 1962, was as a Lord in waiting and whip; he was 33. Since then, he has acquired more experience than most people in

attempting to steer Conservative legislation through the Lords, which is not as easy as it sounds. In fact the idea that 'the Conservative majority can sweep through anything' is 'absolute nonsense'. So, according to Lord Ferrers, is the notion that a Conservative government can 'bus in a whole lot of backwoodsmen'. An attempt to do so might well backfire: 'When peers do come, there is the disadvantage of them listening to the argument and making up their own minds. In the House of Commons they tend to be drafted, like cows, through the milking parlour one way or another.' But even Lord Ferrers admits that 'the call was put out' over the sale of military housing in 1993. 'Negotiations with a potential contractor were three-quarters

of the way through, when somebody attached an amendment to a bill that had nothing to do with housing which would have jiggered the whole thing. That would have deeply frustrated the negotiations. If they had had to be resurrected, the likelihood was that the price obtained would have been far less.'

One of the strengths of the House of Lords, says this man who has been so much part of the political process, is that it is not full of politicians. Peers are the richer – in all senses – for their other interests. 'When people aren't there, they are getting the experience of life that they can contribute to matters when they are being discussed.' Lord Ferrers has had directorships, but the background to his life is Ditchingham

Hall, in Norfolk, where he raises a herd of the Chartley cattle that have been associated with his family for centuries.

The title Earl Ferrers was created in 1711. The first earl, a soldier and courtier, was described by Macky in his *Characters* as 'a very honest man; a lover of his country; a great improver of gardening and parking; a keen sportsman; never yet was in business, but is very capable; a tall fair man, towards 60 years old.' In a lot of which he is followed by the present Lord Ferrers, who is the thirteenth earl. With this family history, it is not surprising that Lord Ferrers takes a long view and has a respect for age in most things, including their lordships. He sees nothing wrong with a senate largely composed of people who are past retirement age. 'If you remove people who are retired and remove the hereditaries, what is left? Only enthusiastic political people trying to climb up the greasy pole.'

Emotionally, Lord Ferrers appears to belong to the pre-Thatcher school of Toryism, inclined to accept that Things Are as They Are. Root and branch measures may lop off unwanted branches, but tend to cut through the roots as well. Not surprisingly, he sees advantages in the presence of the hereditary peers, for whom he himself is such an advertisement: 'They don't bring very much power, but a certain amount of influence.' In an imperfect world, the House of Lords is not such a bad institution, he seems to imply. Reformers would do well to remember the distillation of political experience, which Lord Ferrers has formulated as Ferrers Law: 'Everything has the reverse effect of that intended.'

appointed – at the age of 36. An uncharitable interpretation might be that the Conservatives were short of working peers. But on occasion youth will out, independent of any pursuit by a party behemoth hungry for talent. Valerian Freyberg, the third baron, is a sculptor outside the House of Lords and a cross-bencher, unaffiliated to party, within it. He succeeded in changing the law over army pensions for widows at the age of 24. Lord Iveagh – who inherited his title at 22 – was 27 when he took a Private Member's Bill through the Lords to give passports to the inhabitants of St. Helena (the bill was blocked in the Commons). They come younger still: the ninth Earl of Craven is only nine (he will not be eligible for a seat, if one still exists for him, until he is 21). The House of Lords' Information Office tells me that the youngest attending member of the House is the tenth Earl of Hardwicke at 27. So youth – though only, it must be admitted, of the male gender.

'We are here because we like being useful,' says Lord Ampthill, for two-and-a-half years the Chairman of Committees (the salaried peer responsible for managing all committee work) in the Lords. 'We don't think we're important, but we do think we're useful.' When forming the Lords committee for the difficult and controversial Channel Tunnel (Rail Link) Bill, which sat through June and July, he could find only one life peer who would do it. The other six members were hereditaries. The fact that hereditary peers are prepared to do work that busy life peers find too time-consuming, tedious or inconvenient is another obstacle to reform. It surprised even senior Labour figures to discover, on investigation, that of the 200 or so peers who perform the work of the House (manning committees, deputizing for the Lord Chancellor on the woolsack and so on) two-thirds are hereditary. If the House is to continue its present function, someone will have to do the job. But who?

LAST OF THE INDEPENDENTS?

For Labour, the obvious problem with the hereditary peers, beyond the invidiousness that they see in the principle, is their disinclination to take the Labour whip. The majority of all hereditary peers is Conservative; of those who regularly attend, the one-party affiliation is much less pronounced, since over 200 sit as cross-benchers. Indeed, the hereditary element is the mainstay of the cross-benches. However, only a handful of hereditaries align themselves with Labour.

The Tories have an overwhelming majority over individual other parties in the Lords. Out of a total of 1,273 members of the House of Lords, they can, in theory, muster as many as 489 peers, of whom 317 are hereditary. By contrast, a mere 157 peers take the Labour whip, a figure that includes just seventeen hereditaries. In addition, there are 68 Liberal Democrats, 325 cross-benchers and 106 of no alignment (that figure includes bishops and Law Lords). The Conservative preponderance, while undeniable, is mitigated by the large number of hereditary peers who never turn up: about half of them. The Leader of the Opposition may now regret that they were not persuaded to take leave of absence, indicating that a peer intends never to attend. This would have reduced the size of the Tory majority and perhaps made the hereditary peers less egregious in Labour eyes. Even so, the Tories do not have an overall majority; the balance of power is held by the cross-benchers.

Two-thirds of the cross-benchers are hereditaries. This is hardly surprising, given that most life peers owe their elevation to political influence. 'The great value of this House is the cross-bench,' says the sceptical Lord Williams of Elvel, veteran of the Labour Opposition front bench. Independence is an orchid among the coarser blooms of modern politics: it would die if handled too roughly by reform. The cross-benchers cherish their independence. They have no leader since, as both their present and last convenor testify, they are not susceptible to being led. It is bad form for one cross-bencher to call upon others to come and vote in favour of a motion he or she is supporting; the correct etiquette is to ask them to come and hear the debate, on the assumption that they will then make up their own minds.

The cross-benches are also the natural home of academics, military figures, former civil servants and other peers who have been appointed on the basis of an outstanding contribution in a particular field. Among them is Lord Jakobovits; as a former chief rabbi, it is, he jokes, the only cross he has to bear. The cross-benchers now face an uncertain future. Their ranks would be devastated by the abolition of the hereditaries. That loss could hardly be supplied by prime ministerial appointment: who is the Prime Minister to be impartial? The tradition of appointing non-political figures as peers because they have been Chiefs of the Defence Staff, cabinet secretaries, university vice-chancellors and the like would have some mitigating effect, but not much. They would vanish altogether from an elected chamber. The modern electorate votes for parties, not for independents. The only independent member in the House of Commons is Martin Bell, elected under extraordinary circumstances, and even the once familiar figure of the independent councillor has all but disappeared from local government. For some elections, Mr Blair's government has begun to introduce a form of proportional representation in which electors vote for a party, not an individual representative. Under this system the election of independents is impossible.

NEW LABOUR, NEW LORDS

Since the general election in May 1997, Labour have created an unprecedentedly large number of life peers, to help redress the party balance. Out of a remarkable 90 new Blairite creations, 37 peers take the Labour whip. In their eighteen years of power, the Conservatives did not treat their Opposition generously. Despite the Tories' existing unassailable majority through the hereditary peers, they created, Labour claim, many more Tory new peers than Labour ones. So when Labour returned to office in 1997 they found they had suffered a net loss of 60 peers from their voting strength. What is beyond doubt is that those left in the Labour ranks were getting on in years. Ironically, without access to much of the youth provided by the hereditaries, Labour's strength in the Lords is older than the Conservatives. This is a consideration for their whips. Old people do not want to sit late into the night; their seniority makes them resistant to party pressure. On taking office, the average age of Labour peers was 70. It has now fallen somewhat, much to the pleasure of Lord Carter, the chief whip, though only to 68.

In general, Lady Hylton-Foster thinks the new Labour intake are a good lot. 'The new type of intake is not the old trades unionist. They have much wider experience of life, and make very good speeches. Some of them are rather long and the House gets somewhat restive.' There are, however, special pressures on Labour peers. The Commons system of pairing, by which an MP can absent himself from the Chamber if he can find an opponent who agrees to do likewise, does not exist in the Lords. This puts Labour peers under a particular obligation to attend, given their scant numbers. Not only attend but, now their party is in power, attend all the time; they cannot know when a vote will be forced by the Opposition. 'Suddenly, Labour peers who are young enough for paid employment find they have to be here full time,' observes Lady Mallalieu. Her own programme, as she accommodates her work as a peer with a high-profile career at the criminal bar (unlike barristers with advisory practices, her cases always demand appearances in court), not to mention home life in Oxfordshire, with its attendant children, sheep, chickens and horses, is titanic. She leaves home at 6.15 a.m., goes into the Old Bailey when the doors open at eight and on some nights will not leave the House of Lords until 10 or 11 p.m. Conversely, with such a large new influx of peers on to their benches, Labour Party managers are somewhat stuck for jobs to give them all. But an under-employed peer can be a troublesome peer. The last thing any government whip wants is for his own side to speak: their priority is to process legislation through the system in the minimum possible time.

The film producer Lord Puttnam is a perhaps surprising example of the dedication that being a peer can inspire. How does he fit it in with the demanding schedules of film making? 'That has been the shock,' he says. 'It has become a case of fitting everything else in with it.' When I spoke to him, he had been a lord for four months; soon his duties as a working peer will be his principal occupation. 'I am not a wealthy man but I have done well. I made a simple judgement. If I was going to have a career working within government I was going to have to fund myself. That is why I sold my house in the country. Happily, there is not one day we've regretted it.' He has not yet learnt all the ropes. Our talk is interrupted when, into what we had thought was Interview Room A, bursts the Bishop of Ripon, to change out of his surplice: we have installed ourselves in the Bishops' Robing Room by mistake. It is a moment ripe with cinematic possibilities. But Lord Puttnam believes he has made his last film; with its young audience, the movie industry is unforgiving to older practitioners, and he has decided it is time to move on. So he has joined what might be called the policy industry instead.

'From the late 1980s I worked within the Labour Party to turn around an industrially-based party, with its heart essentially in mass employment and big industry. I worked on an agenda which believed the twenty-first century would be about brain not brawn. Once this concept had found its way into the manifesto, there was an inevitability that anyone who was prepared to give up time to pursuing that agenda would be asked to play an active role.' It will not take him long to find his way around. A member of the Athenaeum, the Chelsea Arts Club and the MCC, as well as the Labour Party, he describes himself as 'a natural joiner'. He does not resent the Tory majority in his new club. 'Part of the esprit among the Labour peers comes from the fact that, technically, we are always outnumbered and have to organize ourselves to deal with that on an almost daily basis.' He has already caught the generous tone of the Lords when he says: 'Most of the votes we have lost were not lost on dumb ideological grounds. I did not necessarily agree with the points made by our opponents, but I felt they had weight and honest intent.'

ALL HUMAN LIFE IS THERE

One of the resources of the Lords is its tribal memory. Some peers have been attending for half a century. Even the officials who serve them tend to have been there a long time. For example, Michael Davies, who, as Clerk of the Parliaments, is the corporate officer responsible for the whole Lords operation, has worked for 34 years in the House. It gives a certain depth of perspective. The title of his office is another indication of the Lords' constitutional supremacy. Soberly dressed, precise in speech, Mr Davies works in a room lined with enormous leather-bound volumes of parliamentary reports. Is it an ivory tower existence? 'I think no one here can be said to have the same strenuous working life that you get in many government departments. The budget that I control is minuscule compared to what many Permanent Secretaries control. We

VALERIAN, THIRD BARON FREYBERG

The place to see Lord Freyberg, a 27-year-old hereditary peer, is in the changing rooms at the House of Lords. This represents the intersection of his two lives, as he throws aside sculptor's overalls and steps into the dark suit of a legislator in the Upper House. At the age of 24, following his maiden speech, he achieved the unfulfilled ambition of many more senior politicians: bringing about a change in the law. This restored the state pension to army widows, previously denied it because they had remarried after their husband's death (as a result of Lord Freyberg's amendment, their pension resumes if their second husband dies). 'To achieve this took six months of full-time work. He has never regretted it: 'I knew I would never have the experience again. I met people of such a mixture of generations and true expertise that not for the world would I have missed having their friendship.'

Earnest, dedicated and articulate, Lord Freyberg is less than half the average age of a peer. What did it feel like to join an institution peopled by men and women of his father's generation, or older? He claims barely to have noticed. 'I have always felt very comfortable here. Everyone has been friendly, unfailingly kind.' He finds it the reverse of moribund: 'What's lovely about this place is that it's alive.' Schooling at Eton may have prepared him rather better than advanced education at the Camberwell School of Art; it is the latter, however, which sets him apart. There is no other sculptor in the Lords. He has to make his living by it. The title was awarded to his grandfather, a Guards officer who, after a brilliant career in the First World War, commanded the New Zealand

army in the Second World War, before becoming Governor-General of New Zealand. Lord Freyberg's father, the second Baron, was also a soldier. So it was natural for Lord Freyberg to take a military theme for his maiden speech. His father, however, took little active interest in the Lords. Valerian explains his motivation in terms of a wish to serve mixed, perhaps, with the understandable desire to experience an institution to which he has access as an hereditary peer, before that access is withdrawn. He sits on the cross-benches.

The subject of the war widows' pensions was chosen at the behest of the

former Labour MP, Alf Morris, now Lord Morris of Manchester, who had met Lord Freyberg's mother at a reception at New Zealand House. Lord Freyberg never imagined that it would have such immediate consequences. The idea that he might change the law was put to him by a member of the Law Society whom he happened to meet as he left the Chamber after his speech. Then began the campaign, which involved a mail shot to all the lords in the House and personal meetings with many of them. He appeared on BBC radio's 'Today' programme and elsewhere. The Officers' Pensions Society

was at hand to help him with facts. As it happened, the Government's Pensions Bill was then at committee stage in its progress through the Lords. Unusually, this Bill had originated in the Lords, which was judged to have more expertise in this area than the Commons. Not all his amendments were accepted, but some were. 'By pure chance, the Bill arrived in the House of Commons just before VE Day. No government could have turned it down.' He acknowledges that his success owed as much to luck as the undoubted merits of his cause, which he described as a 'debt of honour'. Implementing it costs the nation £45 million a year.

'Fortunately I have a filing cabinet, so I can keep most of my papers in the building,' he says in tribute to the resources made available to peers. 'I also have a locker in which to keep my computer.' With his visual awareness, he loves the ambience of the House – 'so overwhelming because the Gothic is everywhere.' He firmly believes that fine surroundings have an inspiring effect on the spirit. 'You arrive here and you are constantly aware of being part of something that has gone on for a very, very long time. You represent the future, but are also aware of the past, where you have come from.' The most difficult thing, for him, is to balance his two existences. Being a peer involves reading, researching, talking to people, writing and making speeches – in short, word-based activities for which contact with people is essential. The life of a sculptor is dominated by emotional and visual responses to the world, often pursued in solitude. 'Going between the two has not been easy. I am constantly changing clothes.'

The former Clerk of the Parliaments, Sir Michael Wheeler-Booth

the cattle disease BSE (bovine spongiform encephalitis), have been of a calibre that could never be achieved in the Commons. Take away the hereditaries from those debates, however, and not only would they often never have taken place (having been moved by hereditary peers) but only half a dozen life peers would have been left to speak in them. At a time when country people feel increasingly misunderstood by the urban majority (and their Parliamentary representatives), to geld the hereditary peers of their right to sit and vote in the House could all too easily be seen by the traditional inhabitants of rural Britain as another blow aimed against them. (It is rather too easy to dismiss these subjects as 'cattle grids in Scotland', in the words of one Labour peer.)

Now, says the Clerk of the Parliaments, the list of special subjects extends beyond agriculture and defence to health, social security and welfare – areas in which the Lords inflicted notable defeats on the Governments of Margaret Thatcher and John Major. The law is another area of interest and there are the twelve Law Lords, to whom much of the Lords' judicial function is delegated. But the arts, too, are strongly represented, not just through the appointment of life peers such as the film maker Lord Attenborough (not a regular attender) but through the enthusiasms of the hereditary element. Many of the latter, for example, like to paint. Lord Gowrie, with his well-known passion for modern art, has been head of the Arts Council as well as chairman of Sotheby's. Other areas of expertise are provided to the Lords by the relatively high number of academics to be found there.

Most aspects of British life find themselves represented somewhere in the House of Lords, but some lacunae are glaring. To quote the Tory peer and agriculturalist Lord Selborne: 'If you were to walk down Brick Lane in the east end [of London] and asked them: "Do you think the second chamber at the moment understands the issues of the first-generation immigrants?", they would say, "No".' Equally, there are as yet few blacks and few Moslems. Reflecting on the Jewish experience, Lord Jakobovits observes that assimilation into the legislative process takes time. He is not disconcerted that, through the bench of 26 Church of England bishops, only one religion – and one denomination at that – is given statutory recognition in the make-up of the House of Lords. 'It does not bother me that as a rabbi I exercise less authority than the bishops. I often wish that the Anglican bishops had more influence and spoke with greater authority.'

have long holidays. Our duties, like drafting reports, have characteristics similar to drafting essays. Putting up constitutional points and historical precedents are possibly like dancing on pinheads. A slight ivory tower existence.' Would Parliament work without clerks? 'Not at all.'

When Mr Davies joined the House of Lords, the subjects most eagerly debated by the Lords were agriculture and defence. Their lordships tended to be landowners, who had served in famous regiments. Proponents of reform still point to the over-representation of landed interest. Approaching half of the lords are landowners or farmers, a figure probably distorted by the number of successful individuals who buy farms in later life. The knowledge that the lords still bring to their discussions of the countryside and wildlife – as well, of course, as field sports – has come to seem all the more remarkable (and precious) because of the urban cast of the House of Commons. These days, few MPs of any party have country roots or list farming among their special interests. So recent Lords' debates on agricultural subjects, including

There are relatively few women in the House of Lords. Part of the explanation lies in primogeniture, though the life peerage has done little until recently to correct the imbalance. There are only 81 female life peers, to add to the sixteen women with hereditary titles. As a woman, Lady Trumpington was not welcomed when she became a peer; when she became a whip, two of the older whips used to walk out of the office every time she came in. Although there are now still only 97 women, out of a total of over 1,200 peers, the showing that the female peers make on both the front benches is strong and Lady Trumpington believes the old prejudice against them has gone.

LET THE TAXPAYERS REJOICE

A marvel of the Lords which would be unlikely to survive reform is its economy. In the context of other great institutions of modern life – certainly the European institutions – it is run on a shoestring. The total budget each year is at present £41 million. This is about one-fifth that of the House of Commons and little less than one-twentieth that of the European Parliament. In almost every respect, the Lords represents value for money. Peers receive no salary. They are entitled to claim a paltry attendance allowance (at the time of writing £34.50 a day), and even when the allowances for secretarial help and accommodation for those living outside London are added, the total per diem is little more than £100. As one eminent life peer commented to me, this just about covers the cost of a room at his club.

There are some peers for whom the attendance allowance represents their only income. And even at the rather modest level at which it is set, it acts as a surprisingly powerful incentive for some peers, including those who apparently could hardly need it (chairmen of City companies and the like), to turn up. But it could not be begrudged: the miracle is that so many able and distinguished people are prepared to undertake the work that they do, sometimes arduous and almost always unnoticed by the public, for so little. In return, they receive the bare minimum of logistical support. But their legislative days are spent in a building of ineffable grandeur: the richness of the decoration, the attentiveness of the doorkeepers, the lingering perfume of cigar smoke in the corridors – everything reinforces the sense that it is a privilege to be there, that this is the inner sanctum of the British establishment.

Few peers have their own offices: even former cabinet ministers have to share. Many peers do not have so much as their own desk. Worse: since the new intake of Blairite peers, Lords Janner and Jakobovits have been reduced to sharing a coat peg. When the Clerk of the Parliaments joined the Lords' staff in the 1960s, peers were 'quite happy with using the library. Nowadays, particularly those who come to us from the House of Commons have got used to their own offices.' In the old days 'members were quite happy to dictate in the corridors: they used telephones in the corridors and so on.' The same conditions now cause disgruntlement. Among new peers, they generate a disbelieving camaraderie. I overheard two working peers – both energetic, one a

household name – discussing a ruse to smuggle cups of coffee to their desks: a practice disallowed by the doorkeepers.

It is difficult to imagine that these homely arrangements, so satisfactory for the taxpayer who funds them, could survive the abolition of the hereditaries. 'It's a part-time establishment,' says Lord Ampthill. In need of some photocopying, Lord Weatherill stands at the Xerox machine himself. A House composed only of working peers would expect the sort of conditions and emoluments usually associated with high-powered jobs. There would soon be pressure for salaries, secretaries and proper offices – which would probably entail the construction of a new building. All of which, it might be argued, the more active of the peers should be allowed under present arrangements. But they are not, and the Lords remains one of the great bargains of modern government. Alas, there is no annual House of Lords Day, marked by a colourful procession of peers through the streets of the capital, to allow crowds of joyous taxpayers to show their gratitude. It is ironic that the only scandal over extravagance in the House of Lords in recent years

An office belonging to one of the few peers lucky enough to have one

has, however unjustly, concerned the redecoration of the apartment of the Lord Chancellor, Lord Irvine of Lairg – Lord Irvine being a standard-bearer for reform.

THE WESTMINSTER RETIREMENT HOME

Neither peers nor MPs retire in the conventional sense; but elderly MPs find themselves making way for younger men, whether they want to or not. Peers, by contrast, remain peers until they die. Of the politicians, most arrive in the Lords only after their Commons careers have ended. Part of the strength of the Lords is the contribution made by people who have retired from their main business in life. This gives it access to the talents of successful people who would have been too busy to attend while still active as, say, the chairman of a major bank. As a consequence, the Lords forms, in the words of an insider, 'a more mature Parliamentary assembly than the Commons. Many of the peers have passed beyond the period of overt ambition'. After all, a senate is necessarily a meeting of old people. (I am grateful to Lord Healey for this: 'Didn't you have a classical education?' he asks.) A retirement age below 95 or 100 would deprive the Lords of the wisdom of such distinguished parliamentarians as Lord Callaghan (86 at the time of writing), Lord Renton (90), Baroness Hylton-Foster (90), Lord Hailsham (91), Lord Longford (92) and Lord Denning (98).

The system is not without obvious flaws, however. Writing in *The House Magazine* (literally the house magazine of the Houses of Parliament), Lord Annan argued that 'a reformed House of Lords must not become an alms home for the aged'. Mentioning this in a speech, he 'could sense a wave of anguish and opposition on the benches, but to point to the occasional Nestor should not, I believe, deter us from making this change.' To the 40-year-old Lord Mancroft, the absence of a retirement age means that seats in the Chamber are sometimes occupied by geriatrics. He tells the story of leading one ancient peer out by the hand, sitting him down in the bar with a glass of water and asking the waitress to keep an eye on him, since he had absolutely no idea where he was. 'You watch great men crumble and die,' he comments. 'That's horrible.'

Peers who have fallen on hard times at the end of their lives sometimes still continue to come, more for the allowances and the free heating than any lingering interest in Parliament. Most peers have stories of them; there may even be one or two around now. They do not speak in the Chamber, and the general view is that they do not do any harm. There is a humanity about the Lords which moves some peers to liken it to a large family. 'The whole secret of the place,' says Lord Ampthill, 'is that we all like each other.'

STRENGTH THROUGH WEAKNESS

By a sublime paradox, the beauty of the present House of Lords, constitutionally, lies not in strength, but in its relative weakness. The Lords cannot impose its views on the Commons, it can only seek to influence it. The hereditary peers in particular are conscious of their strictly limited role. All of this can seem bewildering to the citizen who encounters the institution without coaching in its ways. The first – and abiding – impression that he or she is likely to take away from that first experience is that it is all very extraordinary. And we cannot deny it – it is.

No one imagines that the House of Lords, as presently constituted, has achieved a state of perfection. But a little serious thought shows how difficult it is to devise an alternative, without starting again from first principles. Those principles – above all, democratic selection – will not seem very attractive to the House of Commons if the result is to set up an Upper House with a will of its own, which could be in opposition to it. Almost any change towards greater democracy, however superficially desirable, will create a Chamber that sooner or later flexes its muscles and gives the Commons a bop on the nose. Imagine a House of Lords elected, perhaps by proportional representation, midway through a government's term. Imagine also that the government was as unpopular as they often are at mid-term. With its hostile majority, the Lords might well try to face down the Commons, on the grounds that it had a more recent mandate from the electorate and was elected by a fairer system.

'WE DON'T YELL'

No constituents. No constituency business. Those are just two of the differences between Lords and Commons: there are many others. For example, the Lords goes about its work in another way from the other House. 'The great thing about the House of Lords is that there are absolutely no rules at all,' says Lord Weatherill. 'We work on conventions.' So points of order rarely arise. 'You can speak for as long as you like, and as often as you like – but you don't.' He describes the Commons, on the other hand, as a 'sublimation of civil war, in which weapons are words and not lethal arms'. Two sides confront each other; Government and Opposition MPs may not stray over a broad red line marked on the floor, a distance which keeps the protagonists two sword-lengths and a foot (30cm) apart. They do not address each other directly, but negotiate through the Speaker. The Speaker acts as chairman, keeping order and calling upon members to speak.

The Lords has no Speaker with powers of order. Peers wishing to contribute to a debate register their name with the whips, and a list of speakers is issued. There is a period before the front benches sum up called 'the gap' (nothing to do with a popular clothing emporium, m'lud) which accommodates lords who have not put down their names in advance. Ironically, this little-regulated system encourages conciseness, since the available time is simply divided between speakers. 'One advantage is that it has taught me to speak much more briefly,' reflects Lord Jenkins of his eleven years in the House. He admits to holding the record for a post-War budget speech of two hours 35 minutes when he was Chancellor, but not otherwise to speaking at excessive length in the Commons. There, however, it is not unusual for senior politicians to speak for half an hour. 'But you can often say everything you want to say, a good deal better, in twelve minutes.'

Peers address each other directly, though euphuistically, with many allusions to 'their lordships this and that', 'the noble lord, Lord Such and Such,' 'the right reverend Prelate the Bishop of Snodsbury' and, for the very grand, 'my noble kinsman'. 'Good manners is really the key to it,' says Lord Ampthill, assessing the distinctive tone of the Lords. 'We don't say horrible things about each other, we don't yell.' There is one time, though, when their lordships do, if not shout, at least mutter loudly. If, at Questions, more than one peer stands up to speak at the same time, the others may indicate their preference by enunciating the name of the peer they would like to hear more of – a primitive but democratic method. Generally, this is not necessary: a stately courtesy prevails, with one peer begging the other to speak first. If, once the audience has cried out, still no consensus is reached, it is left to the Leader of the House to choose who will go first. It can be all very baffling to a new-comer like Lord Hurd. 'You never know when you are going to make a speech. In the Commons there is the Speaker who calls you. There is no equivalent in the Lords; you just get up. If three or four peers get up, there is a real awkwardness. Sometimes they mutter who they want to listen to.' He chuckles with embarrassment: 'It is a very awkward business.' Above all, the tone of the Lords is that of being 'immensely polite. It is no good being in a hurry. You just move into a different atmosphere. When the carpet changes from the green of the Commons to the red of the Lords, you are moving into a different civilization.'

Lord Weatherill, convenor of the cross-bench peers and a former Speaker of the House of Commons, is in a better position than most people to compare the level of argument in both Houses. 'I think the level of our debates [in the Lords] is infinitely higher than it is in the Commons,' he says. 'Infinitely.' Having spent 52 years in the Lords, Lord Longford, aged 92, may be accused of partiality. Nevertheless, his verdict is emphatic. 'As an advisory body the House of Lords is unri-valled, the best in the world,' he declares unequivocally. 'It has the best

In the printed papers office

A detail from The Home Rule Debate 1893, *(showing the bishops) by Dickinson and Foster*

debates in the world but the worst system of appointment.' A glance at any issue of Hansard shows that the party political point-scoring by which House of Commons debates are incessantly interrupted is almost wholly absent from the Lords.

Some wonder whether the numbers of peers now attending the Lords will cause its amiable and gentlemanly debating procedures to break down. 'Today for the first time I wondered how long we could go on without a chairman,' said Lord Russell, son of the philosopher Bertrand Russell, after a session which another peer characterized as 'scratchy'. Shortly after this, he astonished the House by interrupting the third reading of the Teaching and Higher Education Bill to move that the Standing Order on asperity of speech be read. This procedure dates from the time before the Civil War when peers really did know about invective. On the present occasion (March 10, 1998), however, the asperity struck non-parliamentary observers as relatively mild, turning on an accusation by the Labour peer Lord Whitty that certain peers had been 'posing to be the students' friends'. (He went on to propound the further enormity that 'It is a hypocritical attitude'.) It was only the third

time the Standing Order had been moved this century. This was followed by a debate, the reading of the motion by the Clerk of the Parliaments and, at the behest of Lord Richard as Leader of the House, a quarter of an hour's adjournment to cool off. 'It is sometimes a noisy House,' observed Lady Hylton-Foster, who can look back over three decades in the House, before this episode took place. 'But everybody still has the same good manners.' Generally, there remains an affection for the old ways, as well as a disinclination to admit of any inadequacy.

More peers now wish to speak than 50 years ago. Lord Longford remembers that, in the 1940s and 1950s, each peer would speak for longer than today; now there is often a time limit on contributions. Again, it is policed by the peers themselves. Those who go on beyond their allotted time are made aware of it by interruptions which, almost invariably, are enough to make the peer in question sit down. The only formal procedure by which a peer can be silenced is what the Clerk of the Parliaments describes as 'the atom bomb to move that the noble lord be no longer heard'. To do so requires a debate, and the debate may simply prolong the agony. It has not been used for many years.

CASTING THEIR VOTES

In theory, peers listen to the debates and then make up their own minds how to vote. That, at least, is the ideal, or myth, to which the less politically minded of them subscribe. The reality is that the Lords has become increasingly subject to the party machine. With it, some say, has come one of the bad habits of the House of Commons: a tendency for peers to say their own piece and then go. This is the behaviour of people who already know how they will vote, because they do so on party lines. Nevertheless, life for the whips who are responsible for getting out their party's vote is not enviable. They have no sanctions to apply to backsliders. Most peers have little desire for ministerial office, so it cannot be dangled before them as an encouragement, and they have no need of more honours. So fewer votes are whipped than in the Commons: until recently a three-line whip had been applied only once or twice in a Parliament. Even newly created peers can have ideas of their own: the Labour vote has not gone up by as much as the number of Labour peers that have been appointed since the election.

One of the newly decorated rooms in the Lord Chancellor's apartments

Lord Callaghan with Baroness Jay, his daughter, the first such double act in the Lords

CLOAKING COMPROMISE WITH POMP

The principal difficulty now faced by the Lords is the increasing volume of legislation bubbling volcanically upwards from the Commons. In the opinion of some peers, it is becoming too great to be given proper scrutiny. This can dishearten people who give their time to the business of the House, because compromises have to be made. But these compromises are the stuff of politics: the very root of the Lords' influence. This, at least, is the view of Lord Cranborne. 'Around about February and March, the business managers look at each other and say: "We are not going to get all this legislative programme through." So the government say to the Opposition: "What about half a loaf?" And they reply: "Three-quarters?"' When the concessions which the opposition extracts are enshrined as government amendments, they will not be reversed in the House of Commons. Lord Cranborne, now Leader of the Opposition, has experienced this system from both sides of the bargaining counter. 'I should think that when I was Leader of the Lords there were several thousand amendments – certainly several hundred – that were put through with gritted teeth.' It is an aspect of our governance that has generally been ignored by constitutional historians.

Horse-trading lacks dignity; all the more reason, then, to bestow an air of *gravitas* through architecture and ceremony. No one could accuse the Lords of selling the public short on such panoply, though it provokes more reverence in some breasts than others. To advocates and detractors alike, it has a symbolic, one might say obsessive, importance. The recent controversy that led to the reform of the introduction ceremony illustrates a central problem of the Lords issue. This ceremony (see page 62) was the means by which new peers, accoutred in parliamentary robes and bicorn hats, showed themselves formally to the House before taking their seats. (There is an equivalent ritual in the Commons, though without robes and hats, and perhaps for that reason little criticized.) The Lords ceremony used to involve Garter King of Arms, wearing his Alice-in-Wonderland tabard, and much bowing, kneeling and doffing of hats. A select committee deliberated on whether it should be shortened. According to Lord Ferrers: 'About fifteen peers took part in the original debate, but by the time the subject had been referred to a committee, who set up a sub-committee which made a report that was discussed by the House, some twelve hours of parliamentary time had been taken up in order to save five minutes of a cherished and colourful, once-in-a-lifetime ceremony. I think the whole thing is absolutely barking mad.' When it was so difficult to reach a consensus about the introduction ceremony, one wonders whether it will ever be possible, not just for the Lords but the country, to agree on what reforms should be made to the institution as a whole.

MUCH VIGOUR, LITTLE POWER

It might be imagined that, on the eve of the third millennium, with democracy in the driving seat and multinationalism attempting to map out the route, such a manifestly British oddity as the House of Lords would be in decline. But not a bit of it. Arguably the House of Lords is now more active than it has ever been. It is certainly more fully attended. When Lord Ferrers first took his seat in the 1950s, the institution was moribund. 'I suppose there must have been only about thirteen, fourteen, fifteen people who really took any interest.' Now, on a Tuesday, as many as 500 peers may attend – though admittedly some go more to watch the performance (and register for allowances) than to participate. In common with the rest of humanity – at least that portion of it living in southern England – the Lords works longer hours

than ever before. Only one parliamentary chamber in Europe sits for more time than the Lords, and that is the House of Commons. When Lord Ferrers was in his thirties, the Lords met on Tuesdays, Wednesdays and Thursdays, and generally finished about 6.30 p.m. Dinner was not served in either of the two dining rooms. It was a rare event for Lord Denham, as chief whip, to announce that, because business was going on so late, 'heavy snacks would be available tonight'.

The change is reflected in today's catering arrangements. There are now five dining rooms, all busy – sometimes crowded – at night. Even so, peers complain of the increasing difficulty of finding a table. 'We have really quite a lot to do,' says Lady Hylton-Foster, with the self-deprecation that is the style of the Lords. 'We grumble tremendously if we have to sit on a Friday, and we have quite a few Fridays coming up.' At present the Labour majority of 179 in the Commons is severely testing the resilience of government support in the Lords, due to the speed at which legislation is being processed through the Lower House. (Unlike the Tories, with their many reserve troops, the Labour peers cannot afford to be absent – and the breakdown of normal relations between the parties, as a result of the threatened Lords' reform, has forced them to attend for far longer than many feel to be reasonable.)

Looking back on her fourteen years on the front bench as a Conservative minister, Lady Trumpington recalls that she was never able to watch television or go to the theatre. 'It is only since the May election [of 1997] that I have been able to go out for dinner with friends.' Generally the burden of work is not of the Lords' own making. It largely reflects the volume of legislation being pushed upwards from the Commons. Each year, peers can pride themselves on moving over 2,000 amendments to Government Bills, 98.5 per cent of which are accepted by the Commons. Given that the Lords is peopled by part-timers, whose labours are rewarded with little more than a pittance, the cheerfulness with which peers of all sides accept the demands made of them is yet another idiosyncracy of the place. That quality would be difficult to replicate in a reformed Chamber, staffed by properly salaried politicians.

So the Lords is at its most active but not, of course, at its most powerful. They cannot raises taxes and, on the face of it, the most damage that they can inflict on Bills passed by the Commons is a delay of one year. Lacking a democratic mandate, they tend to eschew conflict with the Commons. To Lord Cranborne, leader of the Conservative peers, the Lords 'works well as a revising chamber. It works less well when it discharges its principal duty of asking the House of Commons to think again.' The Conservative majority in the Lords gives him a particular incentive to wish the Lords would take a more bullish attitude towards the Commons. He says, though, that this is not a matter of party advantage: democracy would benefit from a stronger Upper House. 'You could argue that a properly reformed House of Lords would have more self-confidence. I do not necessarily think that it would be any better as a revising chamber.'

The Lords can still, on occasion, pack a punch. In the 1980s and 1990s, that punch was delivered where, perhaps, it was least expected, to the jaw of Conservative administrations. It would be too much to say that it had the Government on the ropes, but it caused them to think twice before – and maybe after – entering the ring. For example, the Lords prevented Mrs Thatcher from replacing the Greater London Council temporarily with a nominated body; they overturned Mr Major's intention to privatize local authority inspection of schools; they threw out many Tory Home Office and Education Bills. Their independence in this respect impresses even critics of the present system. 'The number of successful challenges to Conservative Government Bills between 1979 and 1997 was surprising,' writes Katharine Quarmby, a former researcher to the Labour Leader of the House of Lords, in a paper for the left-wing Institute for Public Policy Research: ' ... successive Conservative administrations were defeated over 200 times, on issues as diverse as the definition of unlawful discrimination against disabled people, the rights of former spouses to a share of the earner's pension, and the proposal to allow national sports events to be broadcast on subscription television channels. There are increasing numbers of divisions as peers become more confident of their role as a bulwark against "elective dictatorships".' Forty per cent of the defeats were suffered by the Conservatives. So far the Labour Government has accepted none of theirs.

To the Conservatives, defeat in the Lords was less embarrassing in itself than the attendant publicity. The received idea that Conservative Party managers can call upon armies of backwoods supporters to issue from remote country houses to secure a vote is not entirely founded in the human reality. Very rarely is such a call issued; it tends not to be well received when it is; and infrequent attenders are less willing to be corralled by the whips than the press sometimes has its readers believe.

Occasions when the backwoodsmen have supposedly descended upon Westminster, stumbling around in search of lavatories or tea room, are bitterly resented by Labour peers; the votes on the Poll Tax and the sale of military housing are cited as prominent examples of infamy. However, most of the votes that are popularly said to have been won for the Conservatives through a supposed bussing-in of back-

woodsmen turn out, on analysis, to have been decided by the crossbenchers, who do not have party allegiance.

Whatever efforts the backwoodsmen may put themselves to, their contribution in the lobbies makes little practical difference to the operation of Parliament. For while the Lords is entitled to reject a Bill from the Commons, thereby delaying it for a year, the convention is that, in practice, it virtually never does. The only example since 1949, when the Commons invoked the Parliament Act, has been the Conservative Government's War Crimes Bill, enabling the prosecution of supposed war criminals 50 years after the event. All shades of opinion united against it in the Lords; it was thrown out but reintroduced the following year – with the disastrous results that their lordships had predicted, in the form of an unsustainable prosecution based on memories of events which took place half a century before. Usually, most of the clauses in Bills that are rejected by the Lords are simply reinstated by the Commons. Not that the whips like it: the process uses up precious legislative time.

IS ANYBODY LISTENING?

There was a time when the proceedings of Parliament were regularly reported in quality newspapers, notably *The Times*, and the Lords received some attention. That has long ceased. Parliamentary reports have been replaced by opinion pieces and Commons sketches, with the overwhelming proportion of coverage being given to remarks of the prime minister, senior cabinet colleagues and their opposition shadows. However, the Lords had what in retrospect seems the good fortune to have been the first of the two Houses to have been exposed to television. For the four years before the Commons were televized, broadcasters screened much more of the Lords than they ever would have done otherwise and, as a result, the quality of the debate became known to a wider public. 'It was our finest hour,' reminisces one peer. The Lords has now retreated from this prominence and it is left, largely, to the BBC radio programmes 'Today in Parliament' and 'Yesterday in Parliament' to make anything of its proceedings. Less than quarter of an hour long, they cannot give more than a few minutes to the Lords each day. This journalistic neglect can be a frustration to peers, particularly those who have topped the bill in the Commons or achieved media stardom in their own right.

Roy Hattersley (he prefers not to use his title outside the Palace of Westminster) acknowledges that the debates are of high calibre, but cannot 'avoid the feeling that nobody is listening'. His remark extends beyond the general public to the government itself. Baroness Thatcher disagrees. 'You may not listen to the debates,' she says tartly, 'but you

ABOVE: *Entrance to the Bishops' Robing Room, where the bishops change into their vestements before entering the Chamber*

OPPOSITE: *Richard Carew Chartres, Bishop of London, in the Robing Room*

THE BISHOP OF LONDON

One might have thought that the 26 bishops in the House of Lords were something of an ornament or luxury. Not according to Richard Carew Chartres, the Bishop of London though. 'Modern conflicts,' he says, 'are often about identity politics.' Often, too, they have a religious dimension. Increasingly, bodies such as the World Bank make moral judgements about moral issues – for example the level of corruption – in the countries with which they do business. For these reasons, if no other, it would be important that spiritual leaders have a presence in Parliament. The Bishop would prefer to see representatives of more religious communities than just the Anglican faith there – but he has no desire for the present bishops to be pushed off their benches.

Twenty-six prelates out of a total of over 1,200 peers is not, after all, excessive. Political parties are not the only mass organizations to exist. In this country, he points out, membership of the Communist Party has at no time ever exceeded that of the Lord's Day Observance Society.

With his stern gaze, imposing physique and resounding bass voice, His Grace is not someone to be contradicted lightly. He speaks fluently, with erudition, and has a clear vision of why the House of Lords needs bishops, and vice-versa. The bishops, who do not necessarily vote as a block, bring independence and keep a watch on moral issues as they arise. Since they have many church schools within their dio-

ceses – 152 in the Diocese of London – they can speak with experience on education. The bishops also bring knowledge of the regions where their dioceses are located. For example, the Bishop of Durham can speak with authority on issues affecting the North-East.

To the Bishop of London, though, the significance of his position in the Lords does not reside only in his own contribution to it, but rather in the broad spread of people, with many different types of experience, to which it exposes him. 'One of the dangers of modern life is that of living in a compartmentalized world' where we only meet people like ourselves.' He does not want the Church to be relegated to a 'ghetto of piety' where it loses touch with

the complexities of life around it. Today, the Bishops are as busy in Parliament as they would have been in the last century. Then, however, they showed greater party allegiance, according to the administrations that had appointed them. This put them at the centre of controversy, and it was probably the reaction against it which caused them to attend less frequently after the First World War. In recent years, their sense of commitment to Parliament has increased as the Church of England has become more engaged with social issues, as expressed in its controversial reports *Faith in the City* and *Faith in the Countryside*. With Lords attendance added to pastoral duties, the modern Bishop is a busy man.

can read them.' Even without much direct reporting in the press, what is said in the House of Lords sometimes permeates public consciousness. That at least has been the experience of Lord Jenkins of Hillhead: 'Speeches can occasionally reverberate slowly, unexpectedly. It is rather like House of Lords' laughter: it takes rather a long time to come.' At 92, Lord Longford, hero of the penal reform movement, would agree: 'People do seem to hear of us, you know.' But then causes such as that of Myra Hindley, which he champions, are bread and butter to the press.

At least the peers, unlike MPs, do not need the media as a means of appealing to their constituents. They have no constituents. To Lord Longford, with his lifetime's experience in the Labour Party, it is one of the great advantages of the Lords. 'They do not need to take account of the public. The public are idiotic, misled by the tabloid press.' Other peers share his opinion. In contrast to the Commons, their lordships can allow themselves more 'enlightened' and 'liberal' attitudes to penal reform and other controversial subjects. They can afford to take a longer view being, largely, above the influence of what one present Labour Government minister calls 'the tabloid trash'.

AFTER THE EXODUS

What would the Lords be like without the hereditary element? The one thing that can be said with certainty is: very different. Unrecognizable, in fact. At present, most people would agree that the hereditary peers, despite the arrival of so many life peers since the Life Peerages Act of 1958 (see page 20), still set the style and tone of the place. Every corridor radiates confidence, ease and authority. Some would add privilege to that list; conversely, the comment which peers, both life and hereditary, have most often made to me while writing this book is that it is a privilege to be there. It is appropriate that a peer's robes should be trimmed with ermine. Ermine, being the tail of the stoat which turns white to blend into the winter snow, is an example of natural camouflage. Similarly, newly created peers have a habit of adapting to their surroundings, going native, soon after they arrive in the Lords. Complexions become more florid, as though to blend with the circumjacent red. Even Labour firebrands seem quickly to assimilate the values of the old.

The architecture contributes to this process, of course. The rich Gothic style is everywhere, consistent and overwhelming. The Palace of Westminster was designed by the man who also created the Travellers Club and the Reform Club: it was the great age of clubs. The House of Lords is the grandest, most exclusive and best-appointed club of them all. It is not quite to Lord Hurd's taste. 'There is an extraordinary

Base of the Victoria Tower seen from the south

amount of gold about,' he reflects puritanically. 'It makes it rather un-English, all that gold. I haven't quite made up my own mind whether it is oppressive or not.' He does not like it, but he acknowledges that the Lords would be a different institution without it. 'The architecture plays a big part in the proceedings, that is absolutely true,' he smiles. 'And so do the fellows in the tail-coats.' One doubts, though, that Lord Hurd would ever allow the elaborate deference of the doorkeepers to go to his head.

To outsiders, the House of Lords is forbidding. Even the redoubtable Lady Trumpington admits to having felt trepidation upon first dining at the long table reserved for the peers. Some of the hereditaries jokingly talk about the Lords as though it were public school; they are the boarders, while the life peers are day boys. There is some truth in the analogy: the boarders most strongly project the ethos of the school and it is for just this reason that the abolitionists want to sweep this part of the system away. They see too much of the public school about it altogether. And too much of the Oxford and Cambridge college, too much of the old regiment, too much of the boardroom as well.

Whatever one thinks of it, the House of Lords has been successful in

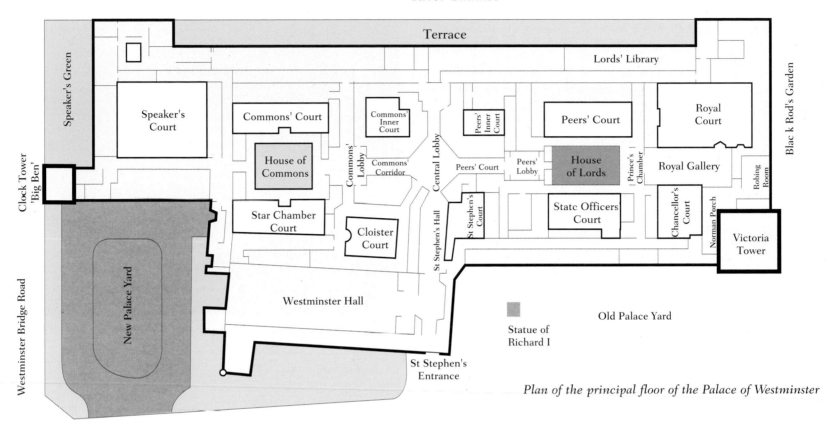

River Thames

Terrace

Lords' Library

Speaker's Green

Clock Tower 'Big Ben'

Speaker's Court

Commons' Court

Commons' Inner Court

Peers' Inner Court

Peers' Court

Royal Court

Blac k Rod's Garden

House of Commons

Commons' Lobby

Commons' Corridor

Central Lobby

Peers' Court

Peers' Lobby

House of Lords

Prince's Chamber

Royal Gallery

Robing Room

Star Chamber Court

Cloister Court

St Stephen's Hall

St Stephen's Court

State Officers Court

Chancellor's Court

Norman Porch

Victoria Tower

Westminster Bridge Road

New Palace Yard

Westminster Hall

Statue of Richard I

Old Palace Yard

St Stephen's Entrance

Plan of the principal floor of the Palace of Westminster

Parliament Square

passing its values down the generations. We live in an age which is not sympathetic to such transmissions of culture. As a result, the collapse of national culture, not just in Britain but throughout the West, is a besetting problem for developed societies. In the House of Lords, it is easy to feel that the possibly anomalous presence of so many peers who are not professional politicians, who do not owe anything to a prime minister or party machine, who regard attendance at the House as both an honour and a duty, contributes to an atmosphere that is specially conducive to public service. At a time when MPs enjoy so little public favour, the different character and motivation of the House of Lords should be regarded, one might have thought, as a national asset. 'Without the hereditaries,' comments Lady Mar, 'it would become a bear garden like the House of Commons.'

And while many of the hereditary peers acknowledge that reform is overdue, it would be wrong to imagine that they would go quietly, unless they were assured that what replaced the present system would be something better. To listen to the youngish Lord Lucas, whose ancestor was killed commanding a troop for Charles I (the title was

Detail of the doorway from the Royal Gallery to the Norman Porch, with statue of Queen Anne

conferred on his widow as a gesture of gratitude by Charles II and descends through the female line), conjures an image of sunlight glinting on breastplates and the wind ruffling the lace collars of cavaliers. Once their death warrant was signed, the hereditaries would have nothing to lose: they could cause a Government no end of trouble in the time remaining to them. Apprehension of this reality has been slow to dawn in the minds of the reform party, but at the time of writing they seem to be just waking up to it.

WOULDN'T DO IT IF YOU PAID US

The great mystery of the House of Lords is why people do it. Most of the peers have homes to go to, businesses to run, activities in the world outside the House. They may be internationally successful architects or film producers, and yet they still believe that they should devote a proportion of their energies to an assembly whose financial rewards are limited, whose debates go unremarked and whose deliberations would often make a tortoise seem agile. From offices fragrant with cigar smoke, the Leader of the House, Lord Richard, is well placed to assess human motivation. 'Oh, a combination of the usual reasons,' he answers laconically, from behind spectacles the size of television screens. 'Service, ambition, enjoyment. A mixture of all those things.' Lord Ferrers has spent a lifetime toiling in the Lords, but rejects talk of this as a political career. 'You don't get a political career in the House of Lords. There are only two cabinet appointments: one is the Lord Chancellor and the other is the Leader. You aren't likely to be Lord Chancellor, and not many people are likely to be the Leader. But there is a job of work to be done, and somebody has got to do it. It is a great privilege to do it.' Lord Longford feels similarly. 'Everyone has only one life,' he says, having chosen to devote his life to work in the Lords. 'One makes what contribution one can.' At the other end of the age spectrum, Lord Freyberg explains his motivation in similar terms: 'You want to contribute as much as you can within the limits of your capabilities.' Lord Cranborne, descended from the nineteenth-century Prime Minister Lord Salisbury, found that lineage scarcely left him a choice. 'I was born over the shop really. If I hadn't been born over the shop, I would have gone off and done something rather more useful.' And even Lord Williams of Elvel admits wryly: 'There are occasions when it is very interesting.'

With his gift for analysis, Lord Russell believes that people come to the Lords for three reasons: 'because they are interested in the business of that day, because they meet old friends and because they like to pick up the news.' It may be that the British gift for snobbery also has something to do with it, though this is strenuously denied by most peers. To them, the prestige of the House is purely a reflection of the quality of

Viscount Cranborne (ABOVE), *former Leader of the House and now Leader of the Opposition, photographed in the Salisbury Room* (OPPOSITE), *which was named after the Prime Minister Lord Salisbury, his great-great-grandfather*

its work. Whatever the case, it is unarguable that the Lords has a mystique which is not accessible to money alone. So plutocrats have something to aim for beyond amassing even more wealth. In comparison to the United States, where society is stratified by earning power, it adds another dimension to national life, which provides variety if nothing else. There is some reason for saying that this keeps alive the public service ideal which has faltered in other areas of existence. 'With privilege goes responsibility,' says that tireless campaigner Lady Mar (who has asked so many questions about organo-phosphate poisoning that she 'couldn't begin to count them'); 'I bridle against injustice and go in with both feet.' It is not a place in which people who have known the blood and thunder of the House of Commons generally thrive. 'The people who love it are the ones from academic life, the military and things like that,' comments the old Commons hand, Lord Healey. 'They have never debated in public.'

There is something in that. At least one peer, as he told me, simply enjoys speaking and believes he is rather good at it. 'You have the pleasure of listening to your own voice from time to time,' admits another. Endless relays of Hansard reporters, each of them transcribing for the ten minutes that is regarded as the limit of human endurance, ensure that those happily chosen words are not lost. The process delights Lord Jakobovits: 'Hansard reprints every word uttered in Parliament the

following day. Where else do you find an instant immortalization of what you say?' There is the thrill of being involved, however peripherally, in the political controversies of the day. But what Lord Selborne calls the 'argy-bargy of the Chamber' is only one side of the activity that takes place in the Lords. It appeals only to certain temperaments and personality types. To others, the quieter deliberations of the committee rooms are a more natural forum.

IN THE GREAT SCHEME OF THINGS

The irony is that reform of the Lords is likely to take place when there is almost no public call for it. We have heard plenty of criticism of Parliament in recent years, but nearly all of it has been directed towards sleaze in the House of Commons. There have been few, if any, allegations of sleaze made against the Lords. This is not to say that it is uniquely saintly in character. By the time someone has distinguished himself, or herself, sufficiently to be made a peer, he or she will have acquired many commercial and other interests; those interests provide the knowledge that enable them to speak with authority. Unlike the Commons, there is no register of members' interests: the Lords speaks on its honour, and this entails the declaration of any interest. As it happens, the Lords' rules are stricter on lobbyists, the subject of so much recent controversy in the Commons. Peers must register any connection with a lobbying firm, and those who do so cannot speak or vote in the relevant debates.

Nevertheless, their lordships' range of activities, not necessarily commercial, can cause ambiguity. Roy Hattersley remembers that on the day he took his seat 'there was a debate on the funding of universities. Was Roy Jenkins then speaking as leader of the Liberal Democrats, or as Chancellor of Oxford University?' Later, the Lords debated the tactics of newspapers such as *The Times* in reducing their cover price to a level apparently intended to bankrupt their competitors: 'of the three people who spoke against amendments on predatory pricing, two were independent directors of *The Times* and one was a *Times* columnist.' Nevertheless, the public remains steadfastly unaffronted by such conflicts of interest, largely, perhaps, because it knows that the Lords has so little power.

When it comes to reform, the Commons must, by any functional analysis, be a more pressing case than the Lords. This is not just because professional politicians have fallen to such a nadir in public esteem. The structure and function of the House of Commons have been thrown into question by Devolution: as I write, the relationship between Westminster and the Assemblies in Scotland and Wales has not been decided. There is also the prospect of greater regional

autonomy in England, and an assembly and a mayor for London. It is impossible to predict what Westminster's relationship to the European Parliament will be in, say, the year 2005. What will be the effect of the single European currency, if it proves a success? Until it is known what form the primary chamber of government will take in the twenty-first century, it seems eccentric to seek to recast that of the secondary one – particularly given the general view that it performs a valuable role, unsung and on the cheap.

As one would expect, Lord Hurd is able to sketch an Olympian view of our embattled parliamentary earthlings. 'The difficulty about the whole parliamentary system is to get involved people who are active and expert. The House of Lords is expert, but it is not on the whole active – people who have been doing. The House of Commons is more and

The Clerk of the Parliaments, Michael Davies

Kathleen Clifford is head wig maker at Ede & Ravenscroft, purveyors of ceremonial robes since 1689 and of wigs since 1726

more just professional politicians with no experience of anything. There is a gap there, which by a quirk the hereditary peers fill, because they are actually active doing things outside politics.' The Lords has a role to play in the present system, and it plays it well enough. However, it is not the role or the playing of it that is at fault, so much as the system itself. 'It improves legislation, but that is not a substitute for having a proper legislative system in the Commons, which we do not have. The quality of stuff coming to the Commons from Whitehall is low and the House of Commons is not equipped to improve it. The House of Lords does do so, but I am not sure that in total that adds up to a good legislative machine. I don't think we have a good legislative machine.' Reform of the Lords, taken in isolation, is not likely to make much of an improvement.

ROUNDHEADS AND CAVALIERS

So much for the grand constitutional issues. What about the wigs and

*Mr Robert Jones and Mr William Stocks, doorkeepers, guarding
one of the entrances to the Chamber*

Coat pegs in the entrance: some peers compare the allocation of coat pegs to life at public school. Heraldry and Gothic decoration provide the peers, even as they remove their overcoats, with a subliminal reminder of their historical responsibilities

cutaway coats and buckled shoes? No doubt the Lords could perform its functions perfectly well without them. But they afford a degree of innocent pleasure to some people, including a proportion of those who wear them. This, at least, is the view of the Clerk of the Parliaments. 'I don't think any of my colleagues in this house would wish to get rid of wigs and gowns. Among the younger ones, if they thought that the wigs and gowns were being abolished they would be extremely disappointed.' The same is unquestionably true of the doorkeepers, in their immaculate formal dress. They would, after all, have to wear some kind of uniform; it might as well be an elegant one. Such details contribute to the general air of stateliness that seeps out of the wallpaper; the oak panelling; the marble washbasins plumbed like the engine room of 'The

Titanic'; the nibs for dip pens in the Library; the Roman lettering on the little black metal flags where cars are parked; the intrusion of technology that elsewhere would be called a video monitor but here goes by the more resounding name of The House of Lords Annunciator.

The Lord Chancellor is reputed to be unhappy in knee breeches, and who can blame him? Still, we rather doubt that the intensity of emotion experienced by people who object to such things is equal to the pleasure of those who enjoy them. Pleasure being the more positive emotion, it ought to win. Others will disagree. It is the sort of question that shows how far the nation – and perhaps mankind itself – still divides into the temperamentally irreconcilable categories of Roundhead and Cavalier. You either like that sort of thing or you don't. That observation can be applied to much else besides court dress in the House of Lords.

WHO ARE THE LORDS TODAY?

As I write, the Lords is composed of 1,275 peers. Of these, 750 inherited their titles from their forebears and only about half this number ever participate in the business of the House or vote. The hereditary peers still reflect the precise gradations of a world ruled by hierarchy. In order of precedence, the Dukes stand supreme (though even they must defer to the Prince of Wales, who never attends the House of Lords), followed by the Archbishops of Canterbury and York. There are only 28 Dukes, including the three Royal Dukes (whose titles were granted because of their close relation to the monarch). Then comes the stately cascade of 34 marquesses, 169 earls, five countesses, 103 viscounts, 406 hereditary lords, 8 hereditary baronesses and three ladies. It will be seen that, as a result of primogeniture, nearly all of them are men, though such are the intricacies of the peerage that sixteen ancient titles can descend through the female line, making, for example, the Countess of Mar a peeress in her own right.

The Countess of Mar's title is exceedingly old, dating, it is said, from at least 1115. Very few peers at Westminster hold titles that are anything like as ancient as that. According to *Burke's Peerage*, just two dozen peers are descended from medieval English nobles. Most of the dukes, all but four of the marquesses and most of the earls have titles that pre-date 1800. But the great majority of hereditary peerages originate from the expansion of Parliament in the nineteenth and twentieth centuries, a handful having been created since the Second World War. Lord Longford is unique in both having inherited a peerage (Earl of Longford, created in 1785) and, before that, having been granted an hereditary title himself (Baron Packenham, 1945). There are four other hereditary peers of first creation (men who have been granted titles that could be inherited by their sons). The Life Peerages Act of 1958 allowed for the appointment of life peers whose titles expire with their death. Since the arrival of the Labour Government of 1965, nearly all new peerages have been of that type.

INSIDE FOR LIFE

There are now (early 1998) 461 life peers in Parliament. Recently, Prime Minister Tony Blair has been creating them at a faster rate than ever before in the Lords' history. Between May 1, 1997 (when Mr Blair won the election) and June 1998, no fewer than 90 have been appointed: so great an intake that their lordships grew restive at the length of the eleven-minute introduction ceremony. (It also raises the prospect of a House of Lords top-heavy with what, in twenty years' time, will have become the Blairite gerontocracy – but Labour aspires to reform it long before that.)

The object is of course to achieve a parity of vote with the Conservatives. But the Conservatives do not have an absolute majority in the House: even taking the non-attenders into account, they could be out-voted by the combined forces of Labour, Liberal Democrats (67), cross-benchers and others, including the Lords Spiritual. The Lords Spiritual are the quota of 26 bishops from the Church of England. In the nineteenth century they were a formidable presence, fluttering like doves in their white lawn sleeves but steely in their opposition to social change. Today the bishops have recovered their parliamentary confidence, after the doldrums of the early part of the century. They leave the Lords on retirement.

THE LAW LORDS

Since the House of Lords is not only a legislative chamber but also the highest court in the land, a number of lawyers have, since 1876, been created life peers specifically to fulfil the legal function of the Lords. Today there are twelve Lords of Appeal in Ordinary, two of whom generally come from Scotland. The designation 'in Ordinary' means that they work full-time and receive a salary, but they are usually called Law Lords. As a group, they embody not only great knowledge but a considerable variety of experience and background. They were all, of course, distinguished judges in other courts before being made Law Lords. Unlike the bishops, Law Lords remain peers for life, though they must retire from their paid work at 70 and nowadays they often retire earlier.

Lord Mackay of Clashfern, the previous Lord Chancellor,
with his train bearer, Nora Dobinson

PRIVATE

HOW THE HOUSE WORKS

Officially, each day's proceedings in the House of Lords start with the Lord Chancellor's procession. It is a little moment of drama enacted largely for the benefit of the peers themselves. There are usually only a handful of visitors milling around the stone-vaulted lobby, with tickets for chairs 'below the Bar' of the Chamber. The doorkeeper calls 'Stand back for the Lord Chancellor'; there is a moment's hush, and the figure of Yeoman Usher, military in bearing, sweeps through an archway, supporting the mace on his shoulder. After him comes another official carrying the Lord Chancellor's elaborately embroidered purse – a mysterious emblem of office, which might be compared irreverently to Mrs Thatcher's famous handbag (the purse, however, is representative of the Great Seal which it used to contain). Then, in a full-bottomed wig, knee breeches, silk stockings and a long gown swept up at the corners, follows the Lord Chancellor himself, looking none too pleased about it: the sort of image of supreme judicial authority that should terrify malefactors and cause householders to bless the Common Law. Finally Black Rod; very rod-like in his military bearing.

They disappear beneath the richly coloured carving of the royal arms, sparkling with gold, and a doorkeeper closes the doors behind them. The ceremony may have its element of human imperfection: what ceremony does not? But as the Lord Chancellor passes he is more than a successful barrister in archaic clothes; for that moment, to the impressionable imagination, the lobby is full of the ghosts of all the previous Lord Chancellors in the 900-year-history of that office. It hardly signifies whether the present Lord Chancellor likes the ceremony (it is widely known that he does not). He could no more escape the heritage of his office than could the Pope.

QUESTION TIME

For five minutes visitors are barred from the Chamber while a bishop reads prayers. Peers turn and kneel on their benches, and I regret to say that some of those who have seen it describe the sight – 'their bottoms in the air like ducks' – with levity. Let us hope their lack of seriousness is misplaced. After prayers, assuming there is no new peer to be intro-

The Lord Chancellor's mace, made of silver gilt and dating from the reign of Charles II. It is a symbol of royal authority

duced, comes Question Time. According to formula, Question Time lasts for exactly half-an-hour and four 'starred questions' are answered; they are called starred questions from the asterisks beside them on the order paper. (An unstarred question, in Lords parlance, means a short debate: the equivalent of an adjournment debate in the House of Commons, only generally, at one-and-a-half hours, three times as long.)

Each question is allowed seven or eight minutes. If the first question goes over length, the later ones must be correspondingly shorter. Peers table their questions up to a month in advance, so the ministers answering them have plenty of notice. But supplementary questions can be asked without notice. In the Lords, unlike the Commons, it is not regarded as good form to try to catch ministers out; they generally have warning of the subjects likely to come up. Another difference with the Commons is that Lords questions are asked of the whole Government, not one particular minister. As a result, it may be that four ministers have to be present.

SHARPENING THE METTLE

In the Lords, ministers tend to have longer experience in office than those in the Commons. They are also expected to answer for every aspect of their department. At present, for example, only one of the seven Foreign Office ministers sits in the Lords, and that is the most junior of them. As a minister in the Home Office, Lord Ferrers 'covered for everything: immigration, crime, drugs, prisons, asylum – and that is quite a thing when you have a Criminal Justice Bill and you suddenly find you have all the Law Lords and the Lord Chief Justice up against you, or with you. There you are, a member of the poor bloody infantry, doing your best.' Is it stimulating? 'It jolly well sharpens your mettle.' The present Government has an exceptionally large front bench team in the Lords, but nevertheless has no minister from the Department of Culture or the Welsh Office. Questions on those subjects must be taken by ministers from other departments. 'The calibre of ministers here is very high,' claims the Leader of the House, Lord Richard. 'People sometimes draw comparisons that are unfavourable to the Commons. They are very much busier than in the Commons.'

I happened to make a note of the questions asked on January 19 1998, when I sat on a plush-upholstered seat, next to Black Rod's box. It was a day picked at random, but the variety of subjects was, in its very

unpredictability, fairly typical. First, the recently ennobled composer Lord Lloyd-Webber wanted to know why VAT at the standard rate of 17.5 per cent is levied on repair bills of listed churches, when new building work is VAT-exempt. This reflects the love of churches that caused him to found the Open Churches Trust. Then the thirteenth Earl of Carlisle asked whether the Government will invite a United Kingdom citizen from an ethnic minority, who has served the nation with distinction, to serve as ambassador in one of the United Kingdom's major embassies at any early opportunity. It emerged that of the 222 Foreign and Commonwealth Office posts throughout the world from which ambassadors are drawn, none is held by a British citizen of Afro-Caribbean or Asian origin.

In the third question, the Countess of Mar pursued her indefatigable campaign against organo-phosphate poisoning by seeking information about the disability living allowance for Gulf War veterans. She was anxious lest the allowance was being unfairly withdrawn from people with chronic fatigue syndrome and other illnesses. Finally, the fourth Baron Avebury – one of the few Buddhists in the House of Lords – urged the Government to draw the prisons in Saudi Arabia to the attention of the United Nations Human Rights Commission. 'That is a delicate matter,' replied Baroness Symons, the object being 'to achieve ... results rather than just make loud noises in the right places.' It happened to be a day on which three of the four peers asking questions were hereditaries though that is not why I chose it. They were all good questions.

HEARING BILLS

After questions, most of the audience rushes out and the unfortunate peer who has to initiate the next debate is generally left holding the floor of a rapidly depleting Chamber. On Mondays, Tuesdays and Thursdays the House proceeds to consider legislation. The Bill before them can be at its second reading, committee stage, report stage or its third reading. Most Bills originate in the Commons, though the Lords shares the burden by initiating some Bills, generally those requiring most specialist knowledge; about a third of Bills start their life here. In the case of Bills that come up from the Commons, the Lords' main job is to make sure the legislation works. This means going through the Bill clause by clause, amendment by amendment, to make certain that the new law really will have the effect intended. Baroness Mallalieu, a barrister, speaks of 'mind-numbingly boring legal debate' – and that, to the outsider, is an accurate characterization of much of the process. It is

Keith Phipps, a doorkeeper, stands sentinel outside the Chamber

necessary because the pace of legislation in the Commons does not always allow sufficient time to be given to the drafting of bills. 'Bills come up from the Commons in a very raw state. The House of Lords is sometimes polishing up a very rough diamond. Who else would do it?' To Lord Jenkins, with half a century of political experience behind him, 'The House of Commons is a very weak legislative chamber. It broadly does what the party leadership, operating through the whips, tells it to.' The arch demonstration of this was the Poll Tax, first introduced and then withdrawn by the self-same Parliament, without an intervening general election.

The Commons operates to a timetable, and governments are forced to cut short, or guillotine, debate to get their Bills through. So not everything in a Bill can be discussed on the floor of the Commons. 'One of the great advantages of the House of Lords is that every single thing that is put down as an amendment has to be discussed,' says Lord Ferrers. 'The last time we had the Devolution of Scotland Bill, it came to us with only seventeen clauses out of 72 having been discussed in the House of Commons. Even the West Lothian question – a wildly controversial situation – had not even been discussed in the House of Commons because they had not got to that point in the Bill.' The Lords, as a self-regulating Chamber, has neither timetabling nor guillotine.

'WE WILL ALWAYS DO WHAT IS REQUIRED OF US'

Because the majority of Bills start in the Commons, the pressure on the Lords invariably increases towards the end of a Parliamentary session, as the legislation requiring their scrutiny piles up. Peers tend to accept the resulting burden as inevitable, and take pride in never being defeated by the volume of work. As Lord Ampthill puts it: 'We will always do what is required of us.' But the progress of legislation is maintained by agreement. 'Last night it was agreed that the House would rise at eleven o'clock in the evening because the House was sitting again today,' comments the Clerk of the Parliaments. 'We don't have the staff to sit until two in morning and then come back again at eleven. For example, the Hansard editors do not leave until at least two hours after the last speech has been made.' Amendments are often grouped into bunches of half a dozen or so, to make the business of debating them easier. But peers are entitled to ignore these arrangements if they so wish.

There is no Speaker to control proceedings. Detailed discussion of Bills tends to attract only those peers specially interested in the subject matter, probably no more than 30 at a time. Thirty is in fact the quorum for divisions on legislation; in other business, including committees it

Mr Skelton, the Head doorkeeper, and his deputy, Mr Crossfield

is three. The Chamber of the House of Lords is not necessarily the best forum for such work to take place, and an increasing number of Bills are considered in the nearby big committee room, known from its 1880s wall paintings as the Moses Room. 'It is much more intimate,' observes an informed source. 'You do not get the filibustering you get in the Chamber.'

It is always acknowledged in the Lords that a democratically elected Government is entitled to get its legislation through. Consequently, agreements can be struck between the parties as to how this should be done. Not that arrangements are always as cosy as this may sound. In the mid-1970s, the Labour Callaghan Government could barely muster a majority in the House of Commons. This put the Tory-dominated Lords in a strong position, and they did not scruple to inflict defeat after defeat on its Bills to nationalize the aircraft and shipbuilding industries and to extend the closed shop of trades unions around docks. In the next session of Parliament both Bills were reintroduced in the Commons under the terms of the Parliament Act, but it did not have to be invoked. The Lords let the Bills through. Since 1949, the only occasion on which a Bill has been passed without the consent of the Lords, as a result of the Parliament Act, has been the War Crimes Act of 1991, under the Conservative Major administration.

For the last twenty years, debates in the Lords have been allocated a fixed time in which to take place. Like everything else, the system is voluntary, the need for it having been caused only by the increased volume of work. Wednesdays are usually reserved for general debates, on subjects of public concern at the moment. Generally they take the form of two time-limited debates of two and a half or three hours apiece. The time available to each speaker is governed by the number of peers who have put their names down to contribute. These debates are not whipped, so the attendance is lower. Nevertheless, as Lord Selborne puts it, they provide 'an opportunity to air issues in a slightly less fevered atmosphere. I think some of the Lords' better moments is when it has taken a quite enlightened view about, say, capital punishment, homosexual laws or even nature conservation. It is difficult to say that at any one moment it changes public perception, but it makes a contribution in a way which is identifiable but difficult to quantify.' A recent outstanding example of the contribution made by the Lords was the debate about beef on the bone regulations, which showed a far higher level of technical understanding than the equivalent debate in the Commons. The Hansard report on this debate was much read by journalists concerned with the issue.

A letter box in the House of Lords. Even later additions have been designed in the Pugin style, and convey an appropriate feeling of permanence

THE COMMITTEES

Probably the greatest development in the work of the Lords has been the proliferation of committees. 'When I began,' remembers the Clerk of the Parliaments, 'there was hardly any structured committee work.' Committees come in three basic forms, which might be called domestic (privileges and procedures), legislative (to consider Bills in order to save the time of the House) and investigative (to enquire into developments that might require the attention of Parliament). There is also the important Deregulation and Delegated Powers Scrutiny Committee which checks all legislation to ensure that ministers are not becoming the modern equivalent of Henry VIII and making laws by regulation without the assent of Parliament.

Most of the numerous committees appointed by the Lords to enquire into subjects of public concern come and go. But two investigative committees are in continuous existence: the Select Committee on Science and Technology and the Select Committee on Europe. The last dates from 1974, the year after Britain joined the (now) European Union. Its object is to consider the legislation, directives and proposals that emanate from the European Commission in Brussels, to gather information about them and to report on those aspects which the Committee considers to merit special attention by the House. The Select Committee on Europe 'has achieved a very high reputation,' says Lord Jenkins, a former European Commissioner. It can marshal a formidable degree of expertise, and the reports it produces are said, at least by the Lords themselves, to be highly respected by our partner countries. It is claimed that no other chamber of any of the other European nations subjects European law to greater scrutiny.

There are no fewer than six sub-committees of the Select Committee on Europe, involving about 60 peers: Economic and Financial Affairs, Trade and External Relations (or sub-committee A); Energy, Industry and Transport (B); Environment, Public Health and Consumer Protection (C); Agriculture, Fisheries and Food (D); Law and Institutions (E), and Social Affairs, Education and Home Affairs (F). Subjects on which the Committee has reported include the protection of personal data, pension rights, Euro fraud, water quality standards and the future of rural society. The Select Committee on Europe has made its remit wider than the equivalent Commons committee because more peers, without the burden of constituencies, are prepared to do the work than MPs. In the judgement of the former Foreign Secretary Douglas Hurd, now Lord Hurd of Westwell: 'It deserves its reputation, which is very high across Europe.' It is something of a happy accident that the Lords retains its authority in Science and Technology.

The Lords Select Committee on Science and Technology began its life in 1979, when the Commons equivalent was disbanded. In the Commons, select committees shadow the various Departments of State. When Science merged with Education to become the Department of Science and Education, their select committees also combined, but Education tended to dominate the discussion. (In 1991, when the Office of Science and Technology came into being, the Commons Select Committee on Science and Technology was restored.) The Lords Committee on Science and Technology had so convincingly proved its usefulness that it continued throughout the period of these changes in the Commons and still operates today.

With its academics, university vice-chancellors, industrialists and science policy makers, the Lords is well provided with potential committee members for Science and Technology. Two of that Committee's five chairmen to date have been Nobel prize-winners. There are sub-committees on anti-microbial resistance in human beings; on the reliability as evidence of digital imaging provided by police surveillance cameras and the like (given that almost anything can now be faked); and on the uses of cannabis. Lord Selborne remembers that when he chaired the Committee on Science and Technology, the supply of expertise exceeded capacity. 'One of my great difficulties was to tell these very distinguished scientists, including at one point a Nobel prize-winner, that there wasn't room for them on the committee. I managed to co-opt the Nobel prize-winner on, I hasten to say, but it illustrates the difficulty.' Since no individual may serve for longer than four parliamentary sessions, the committee membership rotates with reasonable frequency. A balance is kept between the political parties, although most academics tend to be cross-benchers.

There are inevitably a lot of scientists on this committee, just as the agriculture committee tends to be dominated by landowners and farmers. Consequently, they are sometimes accused of going native, or being too closely associated with the science lobby or with farming interests. It is the job of the chairman to find a balance of people who are neutral towards the subject areas investigated. Once the committees have reported, the government must respond within three months; this is followed by a debate on the floor of the House. A good chairman then keeps a watching brief on subsequent developments. But the usefulness of the committees does not stop there. As Lord Selborne explains: 'The virtue of these committees is that their findings have to be published, so even if you do not think much of their lordships' views on these subjects you do, at the end, get a volume of evidence, which is a very good reference point for people who want to follow these subjects up.' The reports are of different degrees of effectiveness in influencing government, and their readership is invariably very specialized. They are none the worse for that.

THE SUPREME LAW COURT

The House of Lords is not only a legislative chamber, but also the highest court in the land. In other countries, it would be called the Supreme Court, hearing appeals from Courts of Appeal throughout Britain (with the exception of criminal appeals from Scotland). Centuries ago, legal judgements were made by the whole House, but as the law became more complex this system broke down. Since 1876 a number of lawyers have been created life peers specifically to fulfil the legal function of the Lords.

Until about 50 years ago, the Lord Chancellor used regularly to preside over the Law Lords when they were hearing appeals. Since then, the Lord Chancellor's department has grown into one of the major spending departments of government, responsible for the administration of the whole court system, so much larger and more complicated than it was in the past, together with the workings of legal aid and so on. So the modern Lord Chancellor does not, in practice, have much opportunity to sit, his position being taken by the Senior Law Lord, at present Lord Goff of Chieveley, who is responsible for the judicial work of the House of Lords and of the Privy Council. To help him is a staff he describes as 'tiny but devoted and very efficient'. The Senior Law Lord is de facto President of the Supreme Court of the United Kingdom.

THE LORD CHANCELLOR

The Lord Chancellor is a member of the Prime Minister's Cabinet. Notionally he is appointed by the Queen, but only in the sense that she appoints the Prime Minister; in practice, it is the Prime Minister who makes the appointment. And yet it would in some ways be wrong to think of the Prime Minister as senior to the Lord Chancellor. In order of precedence, the Lord Chancellor comes, after the royal family, second only to the Archbishop of Canterbury: he is, therefore, a couple of places ahead of the prime minister. There is a certain fitness in this dispensation. The office of Lord Chancellor – or to use the full form, Lord High Chancellor of Great Britain – can be traced back for nearly a thousand years. He is, in effect, Speaker of the Senior House in Parliament which, in the hierarchy of the constitution, puts him ahead of the individual who leads the party in power. Furthermore, his powers are extraordinarily and uniquely wide-ranging since, in addition to his responsibilities in Cabinet and the House of Lords, he is also the head of the judiciary. Occasionally he acts as a judge. His department employs 10,000 civil servants, with a proportionately vast budget.

In their excellent booklet on the Lord Chancellor, published by HMSO in 1977, Maurice Bond and David Beamish describe the origins of the office in the Norman court. The very first reference to a royal

The Lord Chancellor, the Lord Irvine of Lairg, seated at his desk, without wig but wearing his jabot.
His writing paper is kept in a Pugin stationery holder

chancellor comes from 1068, long before Parliament was established. His main duty was one familiar to generations of secretaries since then: the sending of letters. The king's letters were authenticated with a seal – this was the Great Seal, and the chancellor became keeper of it. At different times, the Keeper of the Great Seal has not been the same person as the chancellor. But in modern times, the two offices became one, and the Seal – or at least the embroidered purse in which it might be kept – is one of the Lord Chancellor's symbols of office, carried before him each day when he enters the House of Lords. In 1677 a thief missed stealing the Great Seal when he broke into the house of the then Lord Chancellor, Lord Finch, because the latter kept it under his pillow. However, he did make off with the mace – and this is the first mention of the other emblem of the monarch's authority. (The culprit, one Thomas Sadler, was soon apprehended and hanged for the offence at Tyburn.)

A contemporary described William the Conqueror's chancellor, Hefast, as 'of scant intellect and moderate learning', but some of the later occupants of the post were very distinguished indeed. They were generally clerics and three of them became saints: Thomas à Becket in the twelfth century, Thomas de Cantilupe in the thirteenth century and Thomas More in the sixteenth century. Originally the chancellor was part of the royal chapel. However, he soon acquired his own staff, responsible, among other things, for making copies of all the king's letters on to Close Rolls and Patent Rolls (Close Rolls were for letters that were closed or sealed, and Patent Rolls were for letters that were open – in Latin, *patentes*). From the middle of the thirteenth century the chancellor's administration, known as Chancery, was housed in its own quarters near the present Chancery Lane.

The chancellor's role as head of the judiciary derives from his responsibility in sealing and sending the king's letters, many of which were about law suits. Medieval chancellors were unhindered by the later separation of powers between judiciary and executive, admired as the salient feature of the English constitution. They effectively ran the country, much as a prime minister does today. Their wings were somewhat clipped after Cardinal Wolsey overreached himself; until then, however, as Erasmus noted, the office was 'attended with regal splendour and power'. Some have accused the present Lord Chancellor, with his richly decorated apartments, of reviving that tradition.

Since the Restoration of 1660, the Lord Chancellor has been expected to attend every sitting of the House of Lords as its Speaker. These days he is assisted by twelve deputies; the present Lord Chancellor is not

The Lord Chancellor's wig, robe and tricorn hat,
placed in readiness for their owner

enamoured of sitting on the woolsack in breeches and full-bottomed wig. (There are those who might recall the description of Lord Chancellor Thurlow (1778-92) in the *Rolliad* as: 'The rugged Thurlow who with silent scowl, In surly mood, at friend and foe will growl.') The Lord Chancellor is not expected to act like the Speaker of the House of Commons, chastizing the unruly and deciding points of procedure. His duties in the Chamber are the formal ones of putting motions to the House ('The Question is that ...'), calling votes ('As many as are of that opinion will say "Content"; the contrary "Not content"'), generally deciding which side is the stronger, but sometimes signalling a division by declaring 'Clear the Bar', upon which those peers wishing to vote file out of the Chamber.

Originally, the Lord Chancellor possessed his own court in Chancery, which he attended as well as that in Parliament. Now his judicial function is confined to the Lords, most of which is delegated to specially appointed Law Lords (see page 38 and below). It used to be his duty to preside over the Court of the Lord High Steward, satisfying the old right of peers to be tried, literally, by their peers. The last occasion it met was in 1935, when Lord de Clifford was acquitted of manslaughter following a motor accident. The public may well have thought that the proceedings had more in common with *Iolanthe* than a serious court of law, as over 80 peers processed from one room to another. Such trials were abolished in 1948.

The Lord Chancellor is always a senior cabinet minister, and the present Lord Chancellor, Lord Irvine chairs several cabinet committees. Nevertheless, his principal role remains the administration of justice. As Maurice Bond and David Beamish explain: 'His department is not fully a Ministry of Justice, since certain aspects of the administration of justice are the responsibility of the Prime Minister, of the Home Secretary, of the Attorney-General, and of the Treasury respectively, but the vast majority of administrative functions in the judicial field are those of the Lord Chancellor.' The Law Commission, the Official Solicitor, the Court of Protection, the Public Trustee, the Land Registry and the Public Record Office all fall within his remit. Modern Lord Chancellors may not run the country in the manner of Cardinal Wolsey, but in other ways his powers have continued to accrue over the centuries. They show no sign of diminishing now. It is Lord Irvine who now chairs the cabinet committee to decide the shape of Labour's proposals for reforming the Lords.

THE ROLE OF THE LAW LORDS

The Upper House's twelve Lords of Appeal in Ordinary (usually called Law Lords) work full-time and receive a salary. The Law Lords also constitute the Judicial Committee of the Privy Council. Once, the

THE RECORD OFFICE

The fire of 1834 destroyed all the House of Commons records before that date, with the exception of its Journals. But the House of Lords was lucky: its records were either stored in the Jewel Tower, across the road, or in parts of the building that were not burnt. As a result, it has detailed evidence of its proceedings from the time that a daily Journal was first begun in 1510 (the Commons was later in 1547).

The archives are prominently housed in the Victoria Tower, one of the earliest purpose-built record repositories (predating the Public Record Office of 1851-66 in Chancery Lane). A tower would not have been ideal as offices in the Victorian period (too many stairs),

and no doubt that was why Barry consigned them there. Nevertheless, the scale of the accommodation indicates the importance that the documents had to the progenitors of the new building. At a time of ferment elsewhere in Europe, the long history of British institutions was perceived as an element in their stability and given emphasis. With half of England's parliamentary documents already destroyed, the rooms in which the remainder were housed were made as fireproof as possible. The doors were of iron, the shelves of iron and slate.

'In the seventeenth century the House of Lords was blessed with a number of very industrious clerks', says

David Johnson, the Clerk of the Records. They wrote up their Journals with care. There are committee books from the middle of the seventeenth century, and judicial material from later in the century, when the House of Lords began hearing appeals. The Record Office also contains the master copies of all the Acts of Parliament since 1497. The volume of archival material reflects the activity of parliament. Consequently, it expands rapidly after the late eighteenth century when an enormous volume of Private Bill legislation was required to build canals, roads and railways, to extend cemeteries and market places and to make other civic improvements. When a

Private Bill was opposed, a select committee was convened to adjudicate, and there are 4,500 volumes of evidence given before nineteenth-century select committees in the Tower. Records of the House of Commons resumed in 1835.

The collection also includes such icons of British history as the Attainder of Catherine Howard, the record of the Trial of Mary Queen of Scots, The Declaration of Breda that preceded Charles II's restoration, The Bill of Rights of 1689 and the Abdication declaration of Edward VIII. After modernisation in the 1950s there are now five and a half miles (8.5 kilometres) of shelves for documents.

Judicial Committee heard appeals from India and all the rest of the British Empire. Today its jurisdiction is more restricted, but still varied, covering New Zealand, a number of independent states in the Caribbean, Mauritius, the Gambia and the remaining Crown Colonies, including financial centres such as Bermuda and the Cayman Islands. The Law Lords spend about half their time on this work. If necessary, retired Law Lords or other judicially qualified members of the Privy Council may be called on to sit with them.

Five Law Lords sit to hear United Kingdom appeals: they form what is called the Appellate Committee of the House. They do so around a horseshoe-shaped table in one of the committee rooms, usually Committee Room One. They do not wear robes or wigs, because officially they are not acting as judges, only as a committee of the House of Lords. Counsel addressing them, in his or her gown and wig, speaks from a lectern in the centre of the room. The Judicial Committee of the Privy Council comprises another five Law Lords, meeting in Downing Street. Judgements of the Appellate Committee are passed in the form of orders by the House of Lords, which necessarily happens in the Lords' Chamber. This is a reminder that the powers of the House have only been delegated to the Law Lords, the high court of Parliament still being the ultimate authority.

One task of the Law Lords is to decide which appeals they will hear; this is done by a committee of three. Leave to appeal is granted only in cases which raise a point of law of general public importance. 'The argument before us varies in length,' Lord Goff told the House of Lords recently. 'Usually it takes two days; sometimes it lasts for only one day, sometimes longer – occasionally much longer – than two days. The cases are of infinite variety. The subject matter ranges from genetic engineering to the circumstances in which life support may be withdrawn; from the feudal land law of Scotland to the rights of the Maori under the Treaty of Waitangi; from judicial review of the exercise by the Home Secretary of his power to determine when certain persons detained for life may be released, to the question of whether execution of convicted murderers in the West Indies may become unconstitutional and therefore unlawful after many years spent on Death Row.' Counsel arguing the appeal are under a duty to cite all relevant cases and authorities. This helps the Law Lords do their work without legal assistants, unlike practically every other Supreme Court in the world.

As with so much of the House of Lords, a striking feature of its judicial work is its economy. To quote Lord Goff: 'The prestige of your Lordships' House may be contrasted with the number of Law Lords. In this country the twelve Law Lords provide, with a very small staff, not only the Supreme Court of the United Kingdom but the Final Court of

Appeal of a number of countries overseas. In Germany, the Federal Supreme Court (the *Bundesgerichtshof*) – which must be distinguished from the Federal Constitutional Court (the *Bundesverfassungsgericht*) – has 123 judges, assisted by a staff of 300.' Not that the duties of the Law Lords stop at their work as judges. They are also called upon to preside over committees enquiring into such varied subjects as standards in public life, anti-terrorist legislation and parliamentary privilege. They are also conscious of their less defined role as ambassadors for the British legal system. 'Let us not forget that the Common Law is the legal system of one third of the population of the world. It is, after the English language, perhaps our most precious commodity.'

Any reform of the Lords will have to take account of its role as the Supreme Court. If it became a purely elected Chamber, new arrangements would have to be made.

BLACK ROD

Black Rod is the serjeant-at-arms to the Lord Chancellor. Some time after Edward III established the Order of the Garter in 1348, the knights appointed an usher to clear the way for them as they processed during their annual festival at Windsor Castle and to keep intruders out of their meetings (the word 'usher' derives from *ussarius*, the medieval Latin for doorkeeper). They gave that man a black wand of office. Two centuries later, when Parliament was becoming more formalized in its proceedings, the need presented itself for a similar functionary. Presumably the Gentleman Usher to the Black Rod, to give him the full title, was not overemployed with his Garter duties, and the choice settled on him. So he migrated to Westminster.

Today, Black Rod may be a picturesque figure in his uniform of cutaway coat, knee breeches, silk stockings, shoe buckles and sword. But he is also responsible for all the administration of the Lords that is not legislative (that falls to the Clerk of the Parliaments). If order needs to be kept, it falls to Black Rod to do it. 'But since no peer has been ejected from the Chamber for inappropriate behaviour since 1870, it is not something I am bracing myself for day in day out,' laughs the present Black Rod, Sir Edward Jones. Still, he would be the man for it: a distinguished ex-soldier (Royal Green Jackets), tall and imposing, 62 years old, but with the fitness of someone whose recreations are all out of doors. To be a really effective Black Rod, a requirement must be to look well in knee breeches and stockings; Sir Edward fulfils that demand to perfection. Beneath him, he keeps a force of 24 doorkeepers, in their uniform of tail-coat, white tie and gilded chain, who ensure that the dignity of the House is preserved. 'They are nearly all ex-servicemen, and they

The rod of office, carried by Black Rod and from which he takes his name

are a highly respected body within the House of Lords.' Disturbances, such as the occasion when, some years ago, lesbian protesters abseiled down from the public gallery into the Chamber, are rare.

One of Black Rod's duties is to organize the ceremony associated with the House. Often he has a starring role in it himself. His most visible duty is to approach the doors to the Commons, have them slammed in his face, then to pound on them three times with his staff, summoning the Commons to hear the Queen at the State Opening of Parliament. The ritual symbolizes the independence of the Commons, who could refuse to admit the monarch's representative if they wanted to. It dates from before the conflict between King and Parliament during the 1640s, but assumed particular significance at that time: the Commons Journals of that era often record it in greater detail than subsequently. There are other ceremonies. Each day that the Lords are sitting, his deputy (the Yeoman Usher to the Black Rod) precedes the Lord Chancellor in procession, carrying the mace, while Black Rod follows the procession. For two of the four nights of the week on which the Lords sits, he must also be on hand to accompany the mace out of the Chamber and close the House up.

Though in theory the introduction of new peers takes place under the auspices of the Earl Marshal, as the Queen's representative responsible for ceremony, in practice Black Rod's office makes all the arrangements. 'We brief people, we provide the robes, we run the rehearsals, we get the blame if it goes wrong.' For a new peer, coming to the House of Lords has something of the first day at boarding school about it. 'You walk in that door, and nobody really pays any attention to you, or takes you under their wing. We go to some lengths in the induction process to ease their passage and make them feel at home.' He tries to ensure that new peers receive a ticket for a guest's place in the Royal Gallery to watch the State Opening of Parliament. (Otherwise these tickets, which are in high demand from peers, are distributed by ballot, though that does not solve all Black Rod's problems. 'You get people complaining that so-and-so has had one four years running. It is an agony.')

Ceremony extends to those one-off spectaculars by which the Lords marks great events. Since Sir Edward became Black Rod in 1995, there have been ceremonies, attended by the Queen, for the fiftieth anniversaries of VE Day and the foundation of the United Nations; for President Clinton and President Chirac; and a dinner given in honour of the Queen by the Privy Council, on the occasion of her Golden Wedding. 'I give the responsibility for stage management to the Yeoman Usher, who happens to be particularly good at it. I would like to think we can lay on a good show. We have to call on all the panoply of state ceremonial: gentlemen-at-arms, state trumpeters.' An unforget-

table occasion was President Nelson Mandela's address to both Houses of Parliament, when 2,500 people packed into Westminster Hall to see and hear him.

Deciding who should get tickets for these events, where they should sit, who the ushers will be and so on, is no light task. When the arrangements were being made for President Clinton's visit, Black Rod found himself stopped one day by the former Speaker of the House of Commons, Lord Tonypandy. 'It has always been my understanding that a former Speaker was treated on a par with former Prime Ministers,' he said, forever conscious of the constitutional symbolism. 'I am sitting in the second row. I should be in the first row.' So it is with other minor issues, even the seemingly trivial ones such as car parking space. 'They cause endless angst.'

Day to day, the never-ending programme of building and repair work absorbs much of Black Rod's time. Since 1992, the Houses of Parliament have been responsible for maintaining their buildings. 'The work varies from the door knob that came off that door last night – someone had to come with a screwdriver and put it right – to major maintenance projects. At the moment we are re-doing the roof of the Royal Gallery and the Chamber. It has been going on for 18 months and I suspect that the great majority of the peers don't know it's happening.' Scheduling work so that it does not disrupt the business of the Chamber requires particular logistical skill, and a member of Black Rod's staff does nothing else. The busy time is during the summer recess. 'At the moment we are trying to solve the problem of the overcrowding of the House ... People have desks in circumstances where you wouldn't put your dog. There are sixteen offices which have eight or more desks.' Altogether, maintaining the House of Lords costs £15 million a year.

Security is another concern. It must be provided to the highest level, and yet leave the peers as much freedom of action as possible. As it happens, all recent Black Rods have been well equipped to meet this challenge, having previously been senior officers in one or other of the armed services. Sir Edward's last job before becoming Black Rod had been as the United Kingdom's Military Representative to NATO, in Brussels. These days, an appointment from the services is by no means axiomatic. The final shortlist of three from which Sir Edward was selected included a policeman and a civil servant.

For one day in the year, Black Rod, whose letters of appointment do not mention Westminster at all, reverts to his position as an officer of the Order of the Garter. That is Garter Day in June, when the knights still walk in procession from the royal apartments in the Upper Ward of

Black Rod knocks on the doors of the House of Commons with his staff,
summoning MPs to the State Opening of Parliament

Windsor Castle to St George's Chapel in the Lower Ward, accompanied by Black Rod in his 'Garter mantle' and chain of office. Sir Edward calls it 'a very, very special day in the calendar. I think it is the best day in the year. They are all the most extraordinary people ... It is only one day a year: I could do with some more of it.'

In the nineteenth century, the office of Black Rod could be highly profitable to the holder. His official salary was relatively modest, but he received fees from the Private Bills that proliferated during the railway age. Until the 1820s, he had a lucrative sideline available in the sale of offices, since Black Rod's staff of doorkeepers and housemaids received fees wholly disproportionate to the work entailed. Then a residence was granted him in the House of Lords (Barry provided an apartment in the new building, but it has been used for other purposes since 1895). Nineteenth-century Black Rods also held office for long periods: Sir Augustus Clifford, a former naval officer, served from 1832 till 1877, pocketing a fortune in fees along the way. Clearly Clifford was thought to have overdone it, since reform followed.

These days the rewards are of a different kind. Within the House, Black Rod is regarded with a degree of respect verging on awe. 'I think the office may be held in greater awe than the reality deserves,' observes its present incumbent shrewdly, 'but I don't do anything to discourage it.' Then there is the unique and unpredictable quality of the job itself. 'When I come to work each morning, I simply don't know what the problem of that day is going to be. Every day is different. When someone knocks on the door and comes in, you think to yourself: I wonder what he's going to ask. It could be anything. People come here to confide in you, to ask you questions – it could be anything at all.' Like so many people in the Lords, Sir Edward regards himself as both lucky and privileged to serve in it.

LEADER OF THE HOUSE

Lord Richard, formerly the MP Ivor Richard, lists one of his recreations as 'talking'. As Leader of the House of Lords (1997-8), he played it down. 'I put that in *Who's Who* many years ago,' he jokes, in his rich Welsh voice, 'I can't remember why.' Perhaps he really has forgotten; equally, pleasure in talking can only have been an advantage. 'The method of politicking here is not dissimilar to the United Nations,' he says, in reference to the years during the 1970s when he was British ambassador there. 'You are trying to create consensus behind policies, agreements or resolution.' But a taste for talking does not mean that he is prepared to give much away. He volunteers no stories of his childhood in the Welsh Valleys, from where he won a scholarship to

Lord Richard, Labour Leader of the House of Lords until July 1998

was making sure the ministers were in the right place, doing the right things, making sure our troops were here when they needed to be for a vote.' Was it difficult for him to persuade the right people to become ministers? 'No. It is hard work for low pay. But if you come to the Lords as a working peer you have to expect that. There wasn't a shortage of people who wanted to be ministers. On the contrary.' One of his team, David Simon, gave up running British Petroleum to become a Minister of State in the House of Lords. It could be described – Lord Richard does so describe it – as 'a slightly odd transition', but the happy fact is that 'he is obviously extremely keen on doing it and does it extremely well.'

Ivor Richard was an MP for ten years but his Barons Court constituency disappeared with boundary changes: no one had expected Labour to win the election in 1974, and it was then that he went to the United Nations. After the UN, Lord Richard returned to his first profession of barrister, then served as a European Commissioner in Brussels. Does he feel as much at home as he seems to be in the Lords? 'I preferred the Commons when I was there; I am not sure I would prefer it so much now. The constituency looms so large: they spend an awful lot of time looking after their constituents. It is very difficult being part of a large majority when you are on the side of the Government. The last thing anyone wants you to do is to speak: they want to get the business through. So I don't think I would find it quite so much fun.'

When he first came to the Lords in 1990, what struck Lord Richard most? Typically, the answer is political. 'The differences between this place and the House of Commons,' he says. 'No rules, no Speaker, nobody shouts at you when you speak. When you speak you have to have something to say. It is a more demanding house in some ways than the Commons is. It is also an extremely polite house. Also, I don't think I had really appreciated the amount of hard work that the House of Lords actually gets through. The way it deals with the minutiae of legislation is impressive: they give legislation a much better examination than the Commons. The fact that nearly all Bills are taken on the floor of the House, which they aren't in the Commons. It means that anyone who is interested in a Bill doesn't have to get himself on to a Standing Committee in order to take part in the debate.'

A surprise move in a Cabinet reshuffle prevented Lord Richard from pursuing glory as the Leader of the House responsible for reform. One of the obstacles along that road was his failure to establish any rapport with his Conservative opposite number, Lord Cranbourne. "No speakers" was about the sum of it. We have yet to see whether the elegant Baroness Jay (nicknamed by her colleagues 'Posh Spice'), the new Leader, will prove more clubbable or emollient.

Pembroke College, Oxford, before being called to the bar. He became a QC in 1971, by which time he was already an MP.

Bullish of frame, dark-suited, wreathed in a spicy aroma of Havana cigar smoke – 'my social conscience demands that I support the economies of small islands in the Caribbean,' he laughs, when challenged on the origin of his cigars – Lord Richard has the mien of one who fits effortlessly into the opulent surroundings of the House of Lords. But Lord Richard has hardly gone native: on the subject of the voting rights of hereditary peers, he is utterly implacable. 'Our manifesto is very clear,' he says bluntly. 'We have been sounding out the other parties to see if there is a basis for consensus for doing it (abolishing the hereditaries and introducing a new system of election/appointment) all in one go. That process of sounding out is still going on. If we don't have an agreement, we will do stage one.' But the halfway house that is left could stay with us for decades? 'I hope not as long as that. I expect about four or five years.'

As Leader of the House, appointed by the Prime Minister, Lord Richard was preoccupied by more than reform. 'My main responsibility,' he says, 'was to ensure that government legislation went through the House. Given the composition of the House, this is not as simple a task as it is in the Commons. I had a ministerial team up here, so a lot of it

But there is no doubt that he still has the hereditary peers in his sights. Paradoxically, he believes they must go for the sake of the constitution: 'The composition of the House is totally distorted by the presence of the hereditary peerage. When the hereditaries go, it will have a greater sense of its own responsibility and its own power. The great inhibition of the Lords in the last half century is the feeling that if it misbehaves, the hereditary peers will be for the chop. If you only got rid of hereditary peers and nothing else, you would create a Chamber that would be more of a nuisance to the House of Commons. It would be bound to be more troublesome. I think in terms of the health of the constitution that would not be a bad thing.' Perhaps Lord Richard, as an old Commons man, has gone native after all.

THE LORD GREAT CHAMBERLAIN

The Lord Great Chamberlain is one of two Great Officers of State, the other being the Earl Marshal. The office is currently held by the Marquess of Cholmondeley, now 37, who inherited it from his father. That is, as he is more than willing to acknowledge, 'very strange, an anachronism in many ways ... Almost like being a witch-doctor in an African tribe.' But an even greater complication is added by the fact that the office is shared between the Cholmondeleys, the Earls of Lincoln and the Earls of Ancaster. It rotates between them, changing families at the death of the sovereign. This extraordinary arrangement results from the office having been left, in the eighteenth century, to two sisters, each of whose male descendants then had a claim on it. 'Before I was able to take it on,' says Lord Cholmondeley, 'we had to have signed letters from about twenty descendants.'

In title, the Lord Great Chamberlain is the monarch's representative at the Palace of Westminster. This means that Lord Cholmondeley, in his red tail-coat with his key of office at the back, is there to greet the Queen or any visiting Head of State. His other duties do not weigh heavily. Once, the Lord Great Chamberlain was responsible for running the Palace, but that burden now falls to Black Rod. And Black Rod is left to get on with it. Officially the Lord Great Chamberlain is responsible for the State Opening of Parliament. 'We have a rehearsal the night before,' says Lord Cholmondeley, 'and it always runs like clockwork on the day.' Occasionally there is a need for Black Rod to consult him on other matters concerning the Queen. But there is little need for Lord Cholmondeley to attend the House at other than state occasions.

Lord Cholmondeley has taken his seat on the cross-benches in the Lords, but has never spoken. 'Personally I don't feel I have any right as

The Marquess of Cholmondeley, the Lord Great Chamberlain, holding his wand of office

LEFT: *Peter Gwynn-Jones, Garter King of Arms, who is responsible for the introduction of new peers and the fixing of their titles*

RIGHT: *Velvet tabard worn by Garter King of Arms probably made for Queen Victoria's Coronation of 1838 and bears the Royal Arms. The King of Arms tabard is made of velvet, a Herald's is made of satin, and a Pursuivant's is made of damasked silk*

a hereditary peer to have a say in the running of the country. So I have never voted. I took my seat at a time when I had not decided that.' When not being Lord Great Chamberlain, he spends his time 'half as a film maker and half looking after the Houghton and Cholmondeley estates and finances.' It is, he says, a 'privilege' to be Lord Great Chamberlain, however archaic it may seem. Soft-spoken and modest, he respects the courtesy of the Lords, even if it seems to belong to another era. He also evidently enjoys the pageantry of Westminster. But not the Pugin. How does it all strike the eye of a film maker? 'Closer to Gilbert and Sullivan than anything, with a smattering of Alice-in-Wonderland.'

FEEDING THEIR LORDSHIPS

A hard day's legislating takes it out of you, and the peers need to be fed. The person in charge of this important operation is the catering manager, Alfredo Bibbiani. Dark, twinkling and tactful, Mr Bibbiani is an Italian by birth, who has worked at the Lords for eighteen years. It may seem something of a surprise to find an Italian overseeing the diet of such a traditionally British establishment as the House of Lords. But he finds that, even here, the boundaries of gastronomic acceptability have been pushed back. He takes a patriotic pride in the new taste for pasta. 'When I first came, grilled and fried plaice had to be on the menu every day. Now there are all sorts of fish that we would put on the menu: sea bass, halibut and so on.' Vegetarian dishes, once unheard of, have come into demand. But he sees nothing wrong in tradition, as long as it can be reworked in a lighter, more flavoursome way. So lamb cutlets and fish cakes continue to feature, as do some of the nursery dishes to which their lordships are inexplicably attached. 'Milk puddings are a nice item to have on the menu because they are very good and very healthy,' comments Mr Bibbiani, understandingly. What is the most popular dish? Dover sole.

The challenge of the job does not just lie in food preparation. Peers tend to eat in a hurry. 'Demand reaches a peak about 1.10 p.m.; everything is geared to rush, rush, rush,' comments Mr Bibbiani. By 2.15, he and his staff can begin to relax: they have probably served about 140 peers and their guests. Then the whole of the peers' dining room is given over to tea. Tea in the House of Lords is justly celebrated for its crumpets, muffins, anchovy toast and various relishes. 'Very traditional and very good,' says Mr Bibbiani, correctly. But it is not without its moments of drama for the catering staff. 'If there is an important speaker or debate, peers tend to stay in the Chamber. Then suddenly, when the main point has been made, they rush out to their tea.' Both at

lunchtime and in the evening, Mr Bibbiani has to predict what events in the Chamber will cause numbers to fluctuate. 'Sometimes we get caught out. It happened a few days ago. We weren't aware that it was a three-line whip: we suddenly had over 100 peers for dinner, rather than 30 or 50. It was a big scramble.'

There are five dining rooms, four bars, a staff restaurant and various rooms for parties and the important banqueting operation (on which Mr Bibbiani relies to meet his commercial targets). For parties and dinners, peers who do not care for the richness of Pugin repair to the Attlee Room, a surprisingly plain chamber, with a modern oil by Michael Heseltine (no relation) of the Thames as the only painting. The staff take pride in the furniture by David Linley. 'Altogether we do about 600-700 meals a day, including the banqueting operation.' Originally there was only one dining room, which did not operate in the evening. Space for the extra dining rooms has been found as and where it could be, but 'I think we have reached capacity in production, really, as we are. We cannot expand any more. If all the facilities are oversubscribed, unfortunately there is nowhere else to go.' Yet the longer hours worked by the House mean that more and more peers need to be fed.

The kitchen is still in the basement, where Barry consigned it. It is hardly a convenient arrangement, and in the past communication

Biagio Lammoglia, dining room manager, making
the final preparations before afternoon tea

Alfredo Bibbiani, catering manager, co-ordinates the peers' dining room from his desk

between waiters and kitchen staff has not always been flawless. Now Mr Bibbiani has installed a chef at the top to relay messages as well as one at the bottom to receive them, so at least they are speaking the same culinary language. Another difficulty is the shortage of space for storage. 'Everything has to come fresh in the morning for the day's requirements.' Military precision is necessary in planning deliveries of just the right quantity of food, at times acceptable to the House. Then there is the problem of temporary staff. Mr Bibbiani employs a team of 71 people in the catering department, but they are not always enough. But the standard recourse of maîtres d'hôtel – to have extra staff sent from an agency – is not so readily available at the House of Lords. 'Unlike any other restaurant operation, where you just phone the agency and say: "I need ten washers-up to come now," here we have to have people who are security-cleared.'

On December 8, 1997, Mr Bibbiani's department staged the largest event they have ever attempted: the dinner given by the Privy Council to mark H.M. the Queen's golden wedding. 'It took place in the Royal Gallery, and we had to extend into the Robing Room to cope with the numbers – 320 people! Although logistically it posed quite a few problems, we were determined to do it. The alternative would have been to employ an outside caterer – no way, no way, no way.' With that spirit, our senior legislators will never go hungry.

THE INTRODUCTION CEREMONY

While researching this book I witnessed one of the last of the old ceremonies by which peers were introduced to the House of Lords. It originated in the Jacobean period. The ritual had come to seem unduly long, given the large number of new peers appointed by the Labour Government since 1997. It was a criticism that has been voiced before, during, for example, Harold Wilson's premiership in the 1960s, which saw another bulk creation of peers. And before that, too. As early as 1653 the Garter King of Arms, Sir Edward Walker, published a tract entitled *Observations upon the Inconveniences that have attended the frequent promotions to Titles of Honour and Dignity since King James came to the Crown of England.* Since the House of Lords was shortly to be abolished for a time, Garter's preoccupation may seem the equivalent of fiddling while Rome burns. *Plus ça change.*

The ceremony was as follows. A procession formed up outside the Chamber, headed by the benevolent figure of Black Rod, his long black

Bicorn hats laid out for one of the old introduction ceremonies

BELOW: *The Gentleman Usher of the Black Rod, General Sir Edward Jones and the Yeoman Usher of the Black Rod, Air Vice-Marshal David Hawkins in ceremonial dress holding the Black Rod and the mace, pictured with their assistants Pollyanne Roberts, Rachel Wilkinson and Claire Bostock*

RIGHT: *Sylvia Marsh and Shirley McVicar, Housemaids. They are twins*

Robes laid out in the Moses Room, before an introduction ceremony

wand resting on his shoulder, and Garter King of Arms, sandwiched into his Alice-in-Wonderland tabard and looking as grumpy as anyone who has to wear such a garment in the late twentieth century might well do. He also carried his rod of office, as well as the new peer's letters patent, signed by the Queen. In theory, they could then have been followed by the Earl Marshal, with his baton, and the Lord Great Chamberlain, bearing his white staff, but these hereditary Great Officers of State rarely chose to attend. Next came the new peer himself (or herself), with his two sponsors, one in front and one behind, all carrying cocked hats and wearing scarlet robes trimmed with ermine. The new peer carried his writ of summons.

They set off into the Chamber, and at the bar of the House each bowed to the Cloth of Estate behind the throne. The procession then did a circuit of the Chamber, bowing twice more. At the woolsack, the new peer knelt and presented his writ to the Lord Chancellor, while Garter presented his patent. The Clerk then read the patent and writ (even though all writs and patents are almost the same). The new peer took the oath of allegiance, and the procession moved off again, with another bow to the Cloth of Estate. The final stage is described by Sir Anthony Wagner, Garter King of Arms, and J.C. Sainty, Clerk in the House of Lords, in a paper read before the Society of Antiquaries in 1966: 'Garter now conducts the peer and his supporters to the bench appropriate to their degree, where at Garter's direction they sit, put on their hats, rise and bow to the Lord Chancellor three times, remaining uncovered after the last bow, while the Lord Chancellor, seated on the woolsack, returns their salutations.' If you were near enough, you could just hear Garter stage-managing the business with whispered instructions.

'The procession then once more passes up the temporal side of the House, bowing at the appointed places as before. The Lord Chancellor shakes hands with the new peer from the woolsack and all pass out of the Chamber.' Some peers had more of a flair for the theatrical aspect of their introduction than others. On a good day, the red robes, Garter's glittering tabard, Black Rod's air of authority, the flourish with which the hats are swept off, the Hogarthian figure of the Lord Chancellor, with a tricorn hat perched improbably on his full-bottomed wig, the sort of growl (halfway between a mumble and a roar) that emanated from the peers at the conclusion of the ceremony – all added to a festive spectacle, carried off with brio. On a bad day, it could be awful. Like other initiation rituals, it had the bonding effect of an experience that every peer had to go through.

It is all too much for Roy Hattersley. 'Absurd,' he says. It took him seven months, after his peerage was announced, to brace himself 'to go through this quite absurd ceremony. You may say that I am a big boy and should tell myself that it only lasts a few minutes, but it is so silly.' Other peers, who were not taking part, found it an irritation to have the start of business delayed by the ceremony. But most new peers would like some means of marking the occasion, which their families come to watch; and to Lady Trumpington it would be a 'pity to belittle the big moment of the person concerned just for our convenience'.

There is also the thought that the ceremony has been taking place for over 350 years. It took its present form in 1621, when James I, himself a somewhat profligate creator of peers, wanted the ancient methods of investiture in the presence of the king and the introduction of barons by writ into the House of Lords to be revised – partly, no doubt, because he did not wish to take part himself. Three and a half centuries is a long time for any tradition to have survived. It has now been so modified that the historic heart has gone out of it. No hats. No kneeling. No writs. Garter remains, at the insistence of the Earl Marshal, but with nothing really to do. To traditionalists it seems a diminution – indeed it is intended to be. They observe that it took five hours of debate to agree the new form, rather longer than the few minutes to be saved off each ceremony.

The opulent fireplace in the Queen's Robing Room: Edward Barry tended to over-egg the custard

THE BUILDING AND ITS DECORATION

'The artistical nucleus of the superb and stupendous whole'

There cannot be many institutions whose character is as inseparable from its architecture as the Houses of Parliament. The building is, itself, a great symbol of the nation, instantly recognizable across the world. That part of it occupied by the House of Lords is so complete in its details, so consistent in style, so insistent in its sense of dignity, and so self-confident in its didacticism, that it would be difficult to imagine that the business of the House of Lords could be done in quite the same way in any other structure. Much architectural endeavour is a combination of idealism and practicality: that is particularly true of the Palace of Westminster. Almost every inch of it, additionally, was intended to project an image of the past on to the minds of people who are legislating for the future. One way to read the building is as an illustrated history of Britain, strongly laced with moral values, national identity and a sense of continuity. And yet it was also praised for its modernity: it was the first great Victorian building – the first *and* the greatest, according to some – designed before Queen Victoria's reign had even begun.

'*C'est un rêve en pierre*,' gasped Tsar Nicholas I. To the French architect J. B. A. Lassus it was 'a fairy palace, a marvel of the Thousand and One Nights.' Maybe. But the story of its construction is one of a 21-year war against bureaucracy, budgets and deadlines. The sheer industry required from the architects of all great Victorian institutions makes practitioners of the present age seem mere pygmies by comparison. Indeed, it was enough to kill some of them. In the case of the Palace of

The west front of the House of Lords, showing the peers' entrance

Westminster, the health of its architect, Charles Barry, suffered and his life was probably shortened by the effort. His collaborator, Augustus Welby Northmore Pugin, worked with frightening intensity, which was in part a reflection of his fanatical personality. He went mad and died aged forty. There is something heroic, something Herculean, in the effort that gave rise to Britain's most famous building. For 150 years it has sustained the paradox of a parliamentary democracy, in which the senior element is selected, in large part, by primogeniture.

A CHILD OF REFORM

In its style, the Palace of Westminster is an image of conservatism, looking back to a golden age of British history. But the present building was also, in several senses, a child of reform. The passing of the contentious Great Reform Bill of 1832 had drawn attention to the inadequacies of Parliament's old accommodation, in a jumble of ancient buildings in and around the Palace of Westminster which no architect had succeeded in sorting out. Both the Commons and the Lords had been crammed with legislators when the Bill had been read, and the physical consequences had been unpleasant. Fresher air was a constant demand of those who attended the old chambers. Over the years, the numbers of peers, as well as the number of MPs, had grown, through measures such as the uniting of the British and Irish legislatures in 1801. A haphazard collection of rooms, carved from the innards of a medieval palace, no longer seemed to suit the image or function of a reformed legislature, which liked to think of itself as thoroughly progressive.

Recasting the architecture of the Palace had proved almost as difficult as reforming the constitution. A select committee had been established in 1831 to consider how St Stephen's Chapel, where the

Commons met, could be improved. The Commons, at this stage, were rather worse off than the Lords, who had been insufferably constricted in their old chamber but who now met in a more spacious, though draughty, hall called the Court of Requests, distinguished by its famous tapestries depicting the defeat of the Armada. Special galleries had to be erected whenever particularly controversial proceedings, such as the trial of Queen Caroline, the Roman Catholic Emancipation Bill and the various Reform Bills, threatened to attract a large attendance. (Debates seemed to have been regarded as something of a public spectacle. 'Every fool in London thinks it necessary to be there,' Charles Greville had commented on the occasion of the Catholic Emancipation debates of 1829.) Architects were consulted two years later but nothing had actually been done, when fate intervened – or, rather, fire did. On the night of October 16 1834, the Palace of Westminster burned down.

Almost symbolically, the origin of the fire had again been an issue of reform. In this case, it was a minor reform, and much overdue. It involved the burning of great numbers of tallysticks that had once been used to record payments to the exchequer. A tallystick is a rod of hazel or willow, notched to indicate the sum paid, then split down the middle, with the exchequer keeping one half and the person making the payment the other. The system dated from the time of William I and, wonderfully, survived until 1826. Now there was a considerable quantity of sticks, and the room in which they were stored was needed in order to provide a temporary home to the newly constituted Court of Bankruptcy. How were the tallysticks to be disposed of? The subject gave the writer Charles Dickens, ever the scourge of archaic bureaucracy, a field day:

 The sticks were housed at Westminster and it would naturally occur to any intelligent person that nothing could be easier than to allow them to be carried away as firewood by the miserable people who lived in the neighbourhood. However, they had never been useful and official routine required that they never should be, and so the order went through that they should privately and confidentially burn.

The place chosen for their incineration was a stove used to warm the House of Lords. The alternative of making a bonfire in Old Palace Yard had been rejected as too alarming to the public. Two workmen were entrusted with the task; later, when talk of a conspiracy was in the air, it emerged that one of them was a former convict and the other an Irish papist. But there is no suggestion that they stoked with anything less

than zeal: indeed, too much. They had been supervised, lest they stole some of the sticks. But neither the appearance of smoke in the Lords' Chamber, nor the unusual warmth of the stone floor, occasioned particular alarm. At 5 o'clock, the deputy housekeeper locked up. An hour later a doorkeeper's wife raised the alarm, by calling out 'Oh, good God, the House of Lords is on fire.' According to *The Times*, it had been a Mr Cottle, then being shown the Houses of Parliament, who had first seen the fire; it was discovered to be burning, with grand appropriateness, 'most intensely in the Lords, next to the throne'.

THE FLAMES SHOT UP

A brisk wind helped spread the fire and the blaze quickly took hold. Police and firemen arrived and soon a crowd had gathered, including the Prime Minister Lord Melbourne and other parliamentarians: not all of their efforts at assistance were appreciated by the professionals. By 7.30 p.m. the spectacle had assumed awesome proportions, with the Lords virtually gutted and the Commons starting to burn. It took only five or six minutes from the fire catching part of the Commons for the whole of it to ignite like a Roman candle. 'The flames shot up to a great height and obscured the light of the moon, increasing, rather than diminishing, the apparent darkness of the night, and contrasting in a striking manner the brilliant light which they threw upon the surrounding objects with the general blackness of the sky.' By now, not only the surrounding streets but the bridges were thronged with 'immense multitudes gazing with mingled awe and admiration on the scene of destruction'. The event, dramatic at any time, was particularly thrilling to Victorian sensibilities attuned to Edmund Burke's aesthetic theory of the Sublime. It presented, wrote *The Times*, a 'spectacle of terrible beauty'.

The old House of Lords in 1829

Flames destroy the Houses of Parliament on October 16 1834: as drawn by William Heath by the light of the flames

There were many artists among the crowds who watched the conflagration. John Constable, with his two sons, looked out from a hackney carriage on Westminster Bridge. J.M.W. Turner, who did not forget his sketchbook, was to paint two versions of the scene. Charles Barry was there. Returning from Brighton, he saw 'a red glare on the London side of the horizon' which he was told was the Houses of Parliament on fire.

Augustus Pugin also stood somewhere in the crowd. He watched the blaze with a kind of triumphant vindictiveness, as what he regarded as the gimcrack recent work of the architects John Soane and James Wyatt went up in flames. His joy at the destruction was mixed with relief that Westminster Hall, an example of saintly Gothic architecture, was unharmed – 'almost miraculous, as it was surrounded by fire,' he wrote to a friend.

 There is nothing much to regret and much to rejoice in a vast quantity of Soane's mixtures and Wyatt's heresies [having] been effectually consigned to oblivion. Oh it was a glorious sight to see his composition mullions and cement pinnacles and battlements flying and cracking while his 2 [s]. 6 [d]. turrets were smoking like so many manufacturing chimneys till the heat shivered them into a thousand pieces. The old walls stood triumphantly midst the scene of ruin while brick walls and framed sashes, slate roofs etc. fell faster than a pack of cards.

'Well, I'm blessed if I ever saw such a flare-up as this before,' one bystander was overheard to say, more prosaically. To which an artisan beside him replied, sardonically, that he never thought Westminster 'would go so near to set the Thames on fire'.

'LET ADVANTAGE BE TAKEN OF THIS OPPORTUNITY'

When the new House of Lords was opened in 1847, *The Illustrated London News* wiped a tear of nostalgia from its eye, in memory of the old structure. 'Breaking up a chain of historical associations is a process always reluctantly performed,' it puffed sententiously; 'men cling to the things of the past with singular fondness, no matter how inconvenient they become in the midst of changed times and circumstances.' Three-quarters of a century later, the great historian of the Lords, A.S. Turbeville, opening his *The House of Lords in the XVIIIth Century,* 1927, eloquently evoked the effect of the destruction in banishing the shades of great men. As the spirit of the old Houses of Parliament passed away on the passing of the Great Reform Bill,

 so also there perished their outward and visible body; and thus there departed for ever the chance of seeing with our own eyes the Chambers where the great statesmen and orators of the eighteenth century made their name. The musty odour of the cushions, the faded trappings, or the very confinement of the space might well have preserved for us something of their atmosphere. But we cannot now look upon the self-same wool-sack on which Somers and Hardwicke, Mansfield and Thurlow sat, or upon the great Armada tapestry which bedecked the old House of Lords, an ornament often referred to in the speeches of peers, and the inspiration of one of the most glowing passages in Chatham's orations. The walls upon which their lordships gazed, the benches upon which they sat, are gone as completely as their wigs, their ruffles, and their knee-breeches.

At the time of the fire, there was less of such sentiment around. Most people who had worked in the old Houses of Parliament regarded the necessity of remaking them, almost from scratch, as providential. 'They rank not among the finer specimens of art,' opined *The Times,* while the fire still smouldered. The next day, October 18 1834, the newspaper returned to its criticisms: 'Two Houses of Parliament much less adapted to their purpose could hardly be imagined.' In the best tradition of *Times* leaders, it rose to a grand oratorical climax:

 Accident (for we are happy to see that, after the strictest inquiry by the Speaker, Sir John Hobhouse, and other authorities, the fire is ascribed to accident alone), – accident has afforded an opportunity, which, however wished for, would probably never have arrived through the process of mere deliberation and conviction: let advantage be taken of this opportunity to show that our taste and spirit in material works have kept pace with the improvements in our legal and Parliamentary institutions.

In other words, the new buildings should be in the best spirit of Reform.

FINDING AN ARCHITECT

Immediately after the fire, the old buildings were patched up as best they could be for the new session of Parliament. The Lords sacrificed its Chamber, given a temporary roof, for use by the Commons, just as it would later, after the Commons was bombed during the Second World War. It decamped to cramped accommodation in the Painted Chamber. These arrangements were a sign, perhaps, of the new ascendancy of the Commons, regarded as the more important, if less decorative, assembly. Responsibility for the necessary repairs fell to the architect who was just about the most hated by Pugin, 'that execrable designer', Robert Smirke. Smirke, though the architect of the British Museum, was too austere, not to say tedious, in his Greek Revivalism to excite much public enthusiasm, and the suspicion of jobbery in government contracts acted against the rapid appointment of any architect to the project without scrutiny. So the commission to rebuild the Palace on a permanent basis did not drop into his lap. Instead, it was decided to hold a competition. The process of competition suited an age which was not only instinctively competitive, but, in the light of Reform, more meritocratic and open in its operations.

Not everyone would have shared Pugin's glee in this bonfire of architectural vanities, but the opportunity to improve the conditions in which Parliament worked was welcomed by many commentators. *The Times* called for 'the erection of a noble Parliamentary edifice worthy of a great nation,' which would provide 'space, form, facility of hearing, facility of ventilation, facility of access, and amplitude of accommodation for *the public* as well as for the members themselves and for those who have immediate business with them.' This could hardly be provided by just patching up the old ruins, though it would not have been so difficult to repair them. Parliamentarians saw the challenge less in terms of architecture, as in deciding what fixed machinery was required for effective government. To choose a suitable architect the Select Committee for Rebuilding appointed commissioners.

Three years after Waterloo, the Duke of Wellington signalled what seemed to be the growing irrelevance of the Lords in typically forthright language. 'Nobody cares a damn for the House of Lords,' he told Thomas Creevey; 'the House of Commons is everything in England, and the House of Lords nothing.' To the Duke and other aristocrats, the Great Reform Act promised little less than a Twilight of the Gods for their lordships. Nevertheless, it reflected the Lords' continuing power to influence events behind the scenes that the commissioners were drawn more from the old world of the aristocracy than the new world of Reform. Lord Duncannon, the First Commissioner of Woods and

Burning of the Houses of Parliament
by J.W.M. Turner
The artist was among the crowd of
thousands who watched the disaster. Here he
shows it from the south side of the Thames.

Works, who would later become the fourth Earl of Bessborough, instinctively turned to the traditional leaders of society to make the decision. There were four of them on the Commission: Charles Hanbury Tracy, MP, owner of the great neo-Tudor pile of Toddington, in Gloucestershire, designed by himself; the Hon. Thomas Liddell, son of Lord Ravensworth, another amateur architect with an enthusiasm for Gothic; Sir Edward Cust, son of Lord Brownlow, who had campaigned for such a commission as this, and George Vivian of Claverton Manor, Bath, a writer of pamphlets about London improvements. All were gentlemen of the old school. As with every competition in history, there were some who said that the jury was rigged.

Certainly the commissioners were the sort of grandees who would have been temperamentally attuned to Barry's architecture, though with a weighting towards the architecturally progressive style of Gothic. They seem, however, to have kept true to the old conception of an architect as a kind of upper servant, rather than a professional man on a par with lawyers and doctors. This may be inferred, perhaps, from the extremely short time – initially only four months – allowed for the preparation of the competition entries. In Francis Goodwin's case, the effort proved fatal, insomnia being followed by apoplexy. Barry, with his team of assistants, worked frantically against the deadline.

The commissioners stipulated that the new buildings should be in the Gothic or Elizabethan styles. This might have seemed mildly avant-garde, had not the associations of the place and of Parliament so strongly tended towards it. In its report of the fire, *The Times* had ventured 'to utter a wish that the restoration of the dilapidated parts may be in a style harmonising with the original building'. It was natural to extend this principle to the rebuilding, as opposed to restoration, of the Palace, now envisaged. Gothic was the national style. Its advocates liked to maintain, wrongly, that we had invented it. Its air of antiquity conformed to what Pugin, in *An Apology for Christian Architecture*, called 'the time-worn buttresses of our constitution'. Elizabethan was rather more of a novelty, but hallowed through having shared its period with Shakespeare, Drake and other heroes. What was seen as the buccaneering individualism of Renaissance England appealed particularly to the Victorians, with their attachment to both enterprise and Empire. 'There is something in the rich asymmetry of the Elizabethan architecture, its imposing dignity, gorgeous magnificence, and quaint and occasionally fantastic decoration, reminding us of the glorious visions that flitted across the imagination of the immortal bard of the same age,' the *Quarterly Review* had written in 1831. The writer's emphasis on irregularity, dignity, magnificence and fantastic decoration exactly prefigured Barry's style for the Houses of Parliament.

Statue of Barry by J.H. Foley in the House of Commons

CHARLES BARRY 1795-1860

When the Palace of Westminster burned down, Barry was in his late thirties and well known to society as the architect of a number of churches in Brighton and elsewhere. He was the son of a prosperous Westminster stationer. While architecture counted more in society than stationery, the standing of its practitioners still had a long way to go. Determined to present himself as a professional, Barry struggled all his life to overcome his background in trade. While it did not make him an entirely easy or likeable individual, it strengthened his will. He soon gave up churches: Gothic was not his forte. This cut him off from one of the biggest sources of architectural work in the Victorian age. So he concentrated his energies on clubhouses, institutions and private houses, many of them very grand. His best-known building was the Travellers Club in Pall Mall, whose style, that of an Italian palazzo, reflected his study of Renaissance architecture undertaken on a tour of the Continent.

Barry's style was more opulent than that of either the Greek or the Gothic Revival; it appealed to clients who were tired of the austerity that had until then been the keynote of fashionable architecture. Princely magnificence and a touch of the warm south were its principal characteristics, expressed by means of 'grandeur of outline' and 'richness of detail'; to which might be added opulence of colour. But Barry could work in other styles – Tudor Gothic, Jacobethan, Scottish Baronial – as occasion, and the client, demanded. In this he was like most architects of his generation – but very unlike Pugin.

A CHALLENGING BRIEF

There were two principal challenges beyond that of organizing many different functions into a single structure, and they tended to pull in opposite directions. First, the site allowed an inordinately long river frontage, which only some degree of regularity was likely to order. Second, it was necessary to retain parts of the old architecture, notably Westminster Hall (interestingly, Barry retained and used far more of the old fabric than other competitors). This suggested a more Picturesque approach. The aesthetic challenge was more than equalled by the technical one of how to incorporate all the facilities expected of the new Parliament. A lot was now demanded of public buildings: they had to accommodate not only public rooms but provision for an expanding bureaucracy. At Westminster, Members of Parliament and Lords demanded the same sort of facilities they could enjoy in their clubs – dining rooms, smoking rooms, waiting rooms and so on. (As any modern peer will confirm, this did not extend to offices.) The volume of paper being produced in official reports required libraries of four rooms, with apartments for the librarians. Increasingly, interest from the press and the public called for galleries from which the proceedings of Parliament could be viewed. The Speaker of the House of Commons and other officials, though not at this stage the Lord Chancellor, were given apartments befitting their status. There was an increased demand for committee rooms of various sizes. In addition, the constitutional role of the monarch had to be acknowledged through the provision of a royal route, leading from the carriage entrance via a succession of richly ornamented rooms to the throne itself in the Lords' Chamber. After all, it remained a royal palace, so the sovereign's approval was critical.

For the preparation of his winning competition design, Barry enlisted Pugin's help. It was not an exceptional act. Recently, Pugin had already helped Barry with the drawings for the King Edward VI Grammar School, in Birmingham. Pugin's contribution was to detail the Gothic ornament and design the furniture. Even in the competition for the New Palace of Westminster, Barry was not the only architect whom he assisted: James Gillespie Graham also made use of his services. In Barry's case, Pugin was an inspired choice, since he provided exactly the qualities Barry lacked: knowledge of Gothic sources and a supreme gift for pattern. Barry's skills lay in form, planning and the organization of a large team of specialists, of whom Pugin was one. To those must be added the personal qualities of determination, even arrogance, that enabled him to see the project through to completion. Pugin could never have designed such a complex building as this; but the ambiguity of various references to his contribution has sometimes led people to suppose that he did. There was acrimony after his death, and eventually

AUGUSTUS PUGIN 1812-1852

At the time of the Westminster fire, Pugin was 22 years old, the son of a draughtsman and already someone of preternaturally strong opinions. Perhaps his experience of life had helped exaggerate his character: in the last two years, his first wife and both parents had died, leaving him with responsibility for an infant daughter. His father, a refugee from the French Revolution, had been expert in the delineation of Gothic architecture. To the young Pugin, Gothic became not only a passion, but a series of principles by which all architecture should be judged. The first of these was truth. If a Gothic building looked as though it was built of stone, if a pointed arch appeared to be load-bearing, then it was. Other styles, notably the various forms of Classicism, he derided as shams.

It was a curious credo for Pugin to have developed, since he had enjoyed designing theatre sets: as much about smoke and mirrors (literally) as any form of architecture going. He was so successful at this line of work that, a couple of years before the Westminster fire, the manager of a Paris opera house offered him a full-time job, which he refused. Pugin's originality derives partly from his lack of formal training in architecture. But from the age of fifteen he had been designing furniture, and more recently manufacturing it. He also made money as an early

Augustus Welby Northmore Pugin *by J. R. Herbert*
This portrait hangs in the Pugin Room of the House of Commons

antiques dealer, plying between his home at Ramsgate and France on buying expeditions in his sailing boat. It was an uncertain way for a young man with a daughter and, soon, another wife to make his living and his solvency was always precarious. This, with his back-

ground, this may have given him a sense of exclusion from the establishment, against whose architectural works he inveighed with such scorn. He was also on the point of converting to Catholicism (which he did in 1835), and this coloured all he did. By idealizing

the Middle Ages, he could demonstrate the superiority of life and society in England before the break with Rome. However, to most people in the crowd watching the Houses of Parliament throw flames into the sky, he was completely unknown.

that of Barry, as the dispute over the authorship of the New Palace of Westminster was pursued by their sons, Edward Welby Pugin and Edward Middleton Barry.

Having won the competition, Barry revised his design, under the direction of the commissioners. He also had to prepare a set of detailed drawings from which estimates could be made. Again he was helped in this work by Pugin. A few of Barry's letters for these estimate drawings survive, revealing his relationship with Pugin. The tone is friendly but professional: neither man had time to waste. One letter, dated October 22 1836, is enough to give the flavour of the correspondence. It begins with Barry regretting that, being away from home, he could not acknowledge by return of post Pugin's drawings for the House of Lords, King's stairs and so on, which 'afforded me a rich treat. They will in all respects answer the purpose most admirably. I can easily imagine the great labour they must have cost you, and, knowing all the difficulties, I cannot but wonder that you have been able to accomplish so much in the time. I am not much surprised to hear your health suffers from excess of application.' He urges Pugin to spare himself – up to a point. 'Do not, however, I beseech you, carry too great a press of sail, but take in a reef or two if you find it necessary in *due time*.'

He continues by detailing the new material he has sent Pugin. Clearly Pugin is expected to work up the details to be applied to Barry's structural drawings; the general theme is set by Barry, but Pugin is allowed plenty of room for invention.

 I send by this morning's mail a packet containing tracings of the grand public entrance and approach to the Houses and committee rooms. They are most wretchedly made by a youngster who is as dull and destitute of feeling as the board on which he draws. They will, nevertheless, I have no doubt, afford you all the data you require. The groining and interior generally of the King's or Record Tower Entrance [now called the Victoria Tower] you may make of any design you think proper. You need not be shackled as to height, but the groin should, I think, be concentric with the arch of the opening of the vestibule at the foot of the King's stairs, which you already have.

The design of this part of the buildings should, I think, be in a simple and massive character, and a pillar in the centre of the tower must be avoided. I am much flattered by your hearty commendation of the plan, and shall know where to look for a champion if I should hereafter require one. Truly it has cost me many an anxious thought and an extraordinary degree of perseverance.

It was all done in a tearing hurry: fortunately Pugin was remarkable for the amazing speed at which he worked. There was little time for the precise attribution of credit, and probably neither Barry nor Pugin were much fussed about it. Barry's original scheme contained most of the elements present in the final one, but squashed together. He must have realized that the density of the plan made it airless. In four months, according to *The Illustrated London News*, he produced 97 series of designs, comprising 1,400 drawings. Barry was not above appropriating ideas from other competitors when revising his design. The expostulation continued until Barry was awarded the commission in the spring of 1836. Not that signing the contract signalled the end of the discussions over the new building. Barry, defending himself against the delays and escalating costs which accompanied construction, maintained that he had been 'called upon to do more than is usual or could have been anticipated'. That was in 1849. By then he had:

 been called upon to remodel the internal fittings of the Two Houses and to vary from time to time the arrangement and appropriations of the Offices, the Division Lobbies, etc. of each House, owing to the changes made in the mode of conducting the business of Parliament and the vagueness and insufficiency of the information afforded for the preparation of the original design, which information upon being reconsidered by committees appointed from time to time during the progress of the works has been found in many instances to be altogether at variance to the requirements. The entire plan and construction of the building has had to be modified and recast over and over again.

BARRY'S DESIGN

The final plan is a miracle of clarity. It is based around two dominant axes which intersect at the central lobby. The House of Lords occupies the southern half of the building, around a series of six relatively plain courtyards. The State rooms begin with the royal entrance, a *porte cochère* (allowing a carriage to deliver its passengers beneath shelter) under the Victoria Tower. From here stairs lead to the Norman Porch (named after intended statues of Norman sovereigns: only their pedestals were completed), giving access into a robing room. This is where the monarch is crowned for the State Opening of Parliament, before proceeding down an enfilade comprising the Royal Gallery, the Prince's Chamber and finally the House of Lords itself. The peers' library and committee rooms overlook the Thames. (The acres of fenestration tend to make them soporifically hot in summer and correspondingly cold in

The 800 foot (244 metre) long river front combines symmetry (with endlessly repeated detail) and irregularity (in the placing of the towers)

winter.) The peers' refreshment rooms – originally there were only two, for peers and their guests – were decently sheltered in Peers' Court, though without a view. The Lord Chancellor occupied offices on the west front beside the Victoria Tower but, unlike other officials, including Black Rod and the Librarian, had no residence within the Palace (the present residence, overlooking the river and Victoria Gardens, was not provided until the 1920s; its 1998 redecoration à la Pugin has caused controversy.)

The genius of Barry's scheme for the Houses of Parliament, as built, lies in its combination of irregularity and symmetry. Its massing, with the square bulk of the Victoria Tower at the south-west corner, the slender clock tower containing Big Ben at the north-west and the forest of turrets and ventilation shafts in between, allows it to compose differently from any angle; that variousness is part of its charm. Equally, though, an impression of extent combined with richness is given through the endless repetition of ornament: windows, coats-of-arms, niches and some 200 statues of kings and queens (Queen Victoria recurs eight times). This allowed Barry to give the building, with its classical plan, a Gothic air, without imposing an ecclesiastical interior upon its users. The river front is, in fact, symmetrical, with a pavilion at either end of an 800 foot (244 metre) long terrace, the centre of which is marked by small towers. The west front combines the different elements of the towers, the carriage sweep to the Commons (called New Palace Yard), Westminster Hall, St Stephen's Porch and, set back, the long facade of the Lords; it is best seen from an angle, as a piece of streetscape. In almost any other country, the opportunity to make a grand formal gesture in the part of the facade fronting Parliament Square would have been seized with both hands. But Barry, with his devotion to the English principles of the Picturesque, seems to have composed his building so that it always looks best seen on a slant. With the west front, however, he had no alternative, because of the position of Westminster Abbey on the other side of the street.

THE BUILDING'S CONSTRUCTION

From the start, Parliament wanted to do itself proud, while spending the minimum it could get away with for the purpose. So Charles Barry battled over budgets and struggled to make his final designs conform to public expectations of economy. So did most architects of great public buildings; they still do. Now, 150 years later, this process of economy is forgotten, and we must be grateful to Barry that he did not leave us a building that seems in any way parsimonious. The Houses of Parliament took twenty years to complete: a perspective that tried the patience of the parliamentarians who occupied it. Towards the end of the project, and before his death in 1860, Barry would be hauled before select committees in order to justify costs and delays. These were not pleasant occasions. Barry appears almost permanently to have been grumpy, answering, wherever possible, in a bare couple of words. He was not above ignoring the directions of the committee, when he considered the quality of his building to be at stake. He got away with it, but only just.

The Lords occupied their new Chamber in 1847. It had taken thirteen years since the fire for work to progress this far. Quite long enough – too long indeed, in the opinion of those who would use it – but scarcely sufficient time, given the delays caused by bureaucracy, for the craftsmen responsible for the building work. It is a tribute to the combined genius of Barry and Pugin – the latter became superintendent of woodcarving – that the House of Lords emits an immemorial air. The whole thing was built at a gallop.

PRACTICAL OBSTACLES

There were many practical obstacles to be overcome. An embankment of the river was needed: eventually this provided the terrace on which Members, Lords and their guests enjoy tea. Sewers had to be laid. The right stone had to be found, which took six months; unfortunately the choice fell upon Anston stone, from the Duke of Leeds' quarry, 'characterised,' as M.H. Port writes in his masterly *The Houses of Parliament*, 'by jointplanes running through the beds, leading inevitably in time to extensive lamination and consequent failure of the stonework. The unmarked stone was frequently not laid in its natural bed, so that decay set in rapidly.' In 1841 the team of over 200 stonemasons was disbanded when they went on strike against an oppressive foreman.

Then the issue of how the new building would be ventilated developed into something of an obsession. Ventilation, or the lack of it, had been a constant annoyance to Lords and Members attending the old Houses of Parliament. The difficulty had been particularly acute in the old Commons, meeting in the old St Stephen's Chapel whose narrow, over-intimate dimensions are preserved in the present St Stephen's Hall (rebuilt above the undercroft chapel). This is the passage by which both Houses of Parliament are now reached from the central St Stephen's Porch (it is to perpetuate the memory of the old debating chamber that St Stephen's Hall is lined with statues of orators in full flow). Having

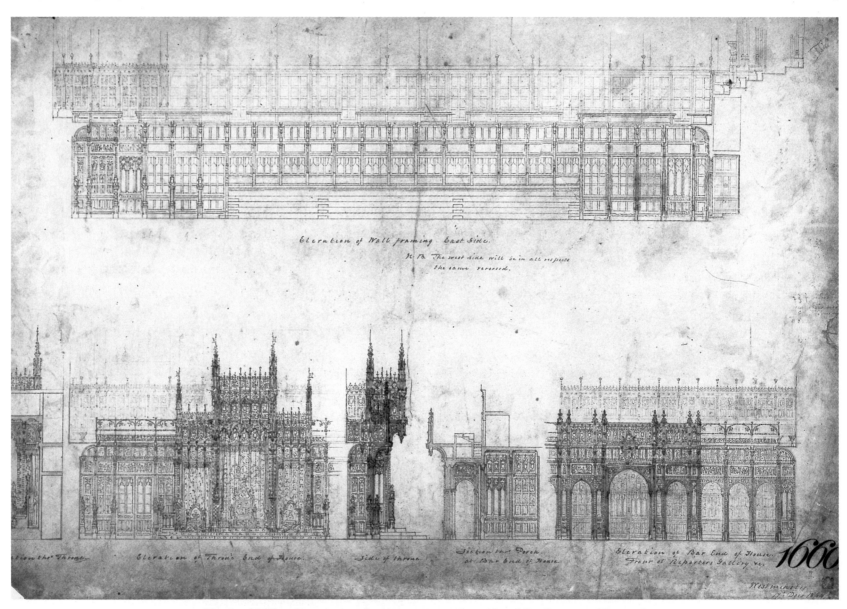

The Lords' Chamber: tracing showing one complete side of the throne and bar end,
taken from a drawing by A.W.N. Pugin dated December 17, 1844

surrendered its Chamber, the Lords' accommodation since the fire had been even less satisfactory. The man appointed by Lord Duncannon, head of the Office of Woods and Works, to superintend the ventilation was Dr David Reid.

Reid was a teacher of chemistry from Edinburgh to whom the ventilation of the temporary Commons Chamber had been entrusted. He was not a professional; in fact he was something of a crank. He was also so difficult as a personality that eventually Barry refused to communicate with him except by letter. Reid's inability to read or to submit working drawings was a source of exasperation to Barry, but Reid was in a position of power. At his insistence, a maze of hidden flues was incorporated into the building, linking in the centre, to expel vitiated air. This purely functional consideration necessitated a central tower, placed over the central lobby, and we must be thankful for the addition. But Reid caused delays (he was an indecisive man); the delays infuriated, in particular, their lordships; and Barry and Reid were frequently dragged before a committee appointed to look into the subject. Eventually, in 1847, Barry was entrusted with the ventilation of the Lords, and they occupied their Chamber that year.

THE CHAMBER

Seeing it, *The Illustrated London News* was moved to hyperbole. 'The Interior of the House of Lords is, without doubt, the finest specimen of Gothic civil architecture in Europe,' it gasped on April 17, 1847; 'its proportions, arrangements and decorations being perfect, and worthy of the great nation at whose cost it has been erected.' The Chamber takes the form of a double cube, 90 feet (27.4 metres) long, 45 feet (113.7 metres) wide and 45 feet (113.7 metres) high. These Classical dimensions must have confirmed Pugin in his famous assessment of the whole building: 'All Grecian, Sir; Tudor details on a classic body.'

The space is organized into three elements. In the centre, to either side, are the tiers of benches on which the peers sit; the Lord Chancellor and the various Clerks sit in the middle, respectively on the woolsack and at tables. At the southern end of the room stands the throne; it was intended that the area around it should accommodate any 'distinguished foreigners' wishing to listen to debates (a practice that has now died out). The northern end is separated from the rest of the Chamber by the Bar. It is here that MPs wait when summoned to the Lords, and where legal counsel stand when addressing the Lords during judicial sessions. The walls are panelled in oak, the carving of which is perhaps the apogee of the Pugin style. The panels themselves are decorated with intricate knot motifs; the ends of the benches bristle

with lively beasts; angels are shown supporting heraldic devices. Between every third panel rises a carved pillar, on top of which sits the head and shoulders of an idealized medieval king. These, like the rest of the most delicate carving, are placed high up, beyond much of the wear and tear inflicted on the woodwork lower down; even so, they are vulnerable to electricians' ladders when light bulbs are changed. This is a working building, not a museum. One of the wonders of the carving is its consistency of style, achieved, apparently, by the employment of young craftsmen who were still flexible enough to adapt to the general style of the workshop.

A gallery with a brass rail runs all round the Chamber, with accommodation for the press in a projection opposite the throne. ('The Reporters' Gallery is most convenient, both in its arrangement and ease of access, the comfort of the gentlemen of the Press having been well studied,' purred *The Illustrated London News* '... From the floor of the House, the appearance of this Gallery is eminently beautiful.' Under the gallery are a series of coats-of-arms of the Lords Chancellor in chronological sequence.) The twelve windows, with their tracery, occupy arches, between which gilded angels project beneath niches containing statues of the barons who signed Magna Carta. Then above everything is the ceiling, covered in pattern and heraldic devices of 'admirable intricacy; and *all* of them are most elaborate in workmanship; indeed, so minute in detail, that an opera-glass is required to detect *all* their beauties'.

With the peers stuffed up in their temporary accommodation of the Painted Chamber, the pressure on Barry to get the Chamber finished was intense. A select committee had been appointed to enquire into the delays in 1843. Barry, always an optimist in these matters, claimed that if he substituted a wooden ceiling for the plaster one originally envisaged, the Chamber would be ready for the next year's session. That was not the end of the delays, but the impatience of their lordships

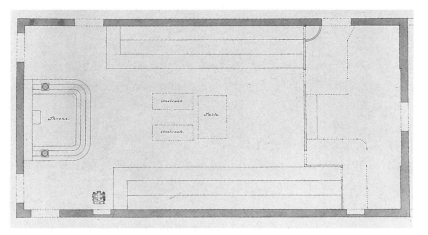

Plan of the Chamber, drawn by William Burn

pressed Barry to hasten construction wherever possible. In 1844 he sought the help of Pugin who had hitherto only worked on the competition scheme. 'Dear Pugin, I am in a regular fix respecting the working drawings for the fittings and decorations of the House of Lords,' he wrote on September 3. '... Although I have now made up my mind as to the principles, and, generally, as to the details of the design for them... I am unfortunately unable to get the general drawings into such a definite shape as is requisite for preparing the working details, owing to a lameness in one of my legs, which has laid me on my back.' Pugin,

A Pugin design for wallpaper incorporating the white hart of Richard II

previously employed by Barry only as a draughtsman, was eventually given an official position as superintendent of woodcarving, at a salary of £200 a year.

THE CHAMBER CEILING

With his *True Principles of Christian Architecture*, Pugin was the enemy of all architectural deceit. Ornament should only be applied to construction: any other approach lacked honesty. There is something of an irony in this. The ceiling that he now prepared to decorate was not the self-supporting structure that it appeared, being suspended from iron

beams above. The roof itself was all of iron, with iron plates instead of tiles being laid on a structure of iron girders. 'The advantages of this material,' wrote the author of a pamphlet on the new roof in 1844, were 'lightness, strength, durability and safety in cases of fire' – the last being, of course, a significant consideration to Barry, with the fate of the old Houses of Parliament in mind. Barry was said to be setting 'a splendid example'. The wooden ceiling hung below this iron novelty. It is six bays long and three bays wide, each bay containing four decorated coffers, themselves subdivided. The bays are separated by what look like massively strong beams, but, when seen from above, they turn out to be hollow. Nor do the magnificent rows of braced arches, springing from between the windows, really bear the weight of the ceiling, as they would appear to do. Rather the reverse: they are actually suspended from the beams they seem to support.

The skill of the carpenters is shown in ways quite different from those of the Middle Ages. No timber much longer than 12 feet (3.6 metres) was used in the whole ceiling. For speed of assembly, simple butt-joints and, at the corners, scribing (rather than mitring) were used. The whole thing was run up in a series of prefabricated sections that were then fitted together in situ. None of this less than perfect workmanship can be laid at Pugin's door, though he must have known about it; nor would it have become apparent had not the state of the ceiling drawn attention to itself in dramatic fashion some 130 years after it was built.

The use of short lengths of timber had not been the only cost-cutting measure. In assembling the timbers, glue, screws and the odd nail were preferred to the more durable, but costly and time-consuming method of jointing. Eventually the glue gave out, leaving nothing to keep the carved wooden bosses on the beams in place. Thus it was that on July 21, 1980, one of these massive bosses, without a hint of warning, detached itself and hurtled towards the red leather benches below, crashing on to a seat normally occupied by the nonagenarian Lord Shinwell. Had the timing been different, it would have summarily prevented the celebration of his hundredth birthday, which took place four years later. Scaffolding was erected and the ceiling examined. It turned out that the condition of the bosses was far less worrying than the condition of the timber itself. Quite large areas had been reduced to a worthless, crumbly state, akin to that caused by dry rot. The sides of some of the beams were so weak that they could be scooped out with a pen. It could have been a combination of gas lights and the iron roof that caused it: the fantastic heat that built up in the roof space during summer may have baked the timbers like an oven. No one knows for certain.

The ceiling radiates with gilding: a revelation when it was restored in the 1980s. To decorate the coffers of the ceiling, Pugin designed heraldic

emblems, carved in the central lozenge, painted in the four other panels. Over the throne is Queen Victoria's monogram, crowned and looped with a cord. Other lozenges show the white hart of Richard II, the sun of the House of York, the crown in a bush of Henry VII, the lion passant of England, the lion rampant of Scotland and the harp of Ireland. Further emblems include the falcon, the dragon and the greyhound. As *The Illustrated London News* describes it: 'Sceptres and orbs, emblems of regal power, with crowns; the scales indicative of justice; mitres and crosiers, symbols of religion; and blunted swords of mercy add their hieroglyphic interest: while crowns and coronets, and the ostrich plumes of the Prince of Wales, form enrichments more easily understood.' The five-sided panels at the corners of the coffers, with their painted ornament, bear yet different motifs: the rose of England, the pomegranate of Castile, the portcullis of Beaufort, the lily of France, as well as the lion of England – along with shields showing 'the fanciful armorial bearings of those countries which ages since composed the Saxon Heptarchy'. The colours are predominantly red, gold and dark blue.

Pugin's favourite painter-decorator, Frederick Crace, was responsible for the painting. 'I herewith send you the ceiling and will endeavour to explain the idea which Mr Barry wished to be carried out,' wrote Pugin to Crace in a letter in the Victoria & Albert Museum. '... I can come to you early on Monday morning next *probably before breakfast*. Could you have some of these badges drawn out only in charcoal for me to see. It would advance things very much. I think you will understand my sketches but I can correct anything if you will get the panels sketched in full size....You may make a capital thing of the Lion passant.'

Despite Pugin's views on the iniquity of mass production, Barry had five of Jordan's patent woodcarving machines set up in the workshops near Vauxhall Bridge. These machines were capable of carving eight copies from one original at the same time. Jordan himself was employed from April 1845 at the same salary as Pugin. The machines could only be used for the cruder work, and all the more delicate carving was finished by hand. Some carvers applied their names to their work, and these were discovered during the restoration: Cotton, Park, Scriven, Browne, Potts, Hatton... Lacey and Nicholls left their names with the date, 1847; so did G. Kett – a forebear of Ratee & Kett of Cambridge. With the names was an inscription indicating the craftsmen's anxiety at getting it all done before the opening of Parliament. 'Sess. begins 5 April

the garter, supporters, helmet and crest, are the royal arms of England. The enrichments of the carving become ever more elaborate as the canopy goes up. The central section of the canopy, higher than the wings, contains five niches, occupied by knightly figures armed, as neo-troubadours liked to express it, *cap-a-pie*. In the centre, St George slays the dragon; to the sides, knights bear tournament shields emblazoned with the emblems of the Orders of the Garter, the Bath, the Thistle and St Patrick. Every inch of the structure is covered in rich carving, ingeniously ringing the changes on the royal emblems of rose, lion and so on.

The form of the throne follows that of the medieval Coronation Chair in Westminster Abbey. About 7 feet (2.1 metres) tall, it is made of mahogany, though you would hardly know it since the exterior is entirely covered in gold leaf. The canopy above it is also gilded. 'The cushioned back is composed of regal velvet of the finest pile bordered with the arms of England,' commented the *Observer*, 'Surrounding the Royal Arms are enamel ornaments in the Byzantine style, alternating with crystals of purest water.' The piece was made, along with important other furniture, by John Webb of Bond Street; Hardman & Co., makers of metalwork and stained glass, whose owner John Hardman was Pugin's friend and colleague, had sent them the crystals and enamels in February 1847.

The Illustrated London News was left gasping. 'As every portion of Her Majesty's Throne, and the Chairs for the Princes, is gilded, some idea may be formed of their excessively splendid appearance; and, standing as they do under a canopy of the richest design, glowing with gold and colours, they produce an effect absolutely bewildering, from its gorgeousness – and certainly no English monarch ever sat upon a throne of such consummate magnificence as this prepared for Her Majesty Queen Victoria.'

THE LORDS' LIBRARY

Another of the high points of Pugin's decorative scheme is the Lords' Library, its atmosphere evoked in a contemporary guidebook:

 Every portion is complete and harmonious and every article of furniture in the rooms has been designed and manufactured in accordance with the architecture, indeed we could fancy ourselves in one of those artistic and Lordly apartments of olden time, once to be found in old mansions of Henry's and Elizabeth's time such as Nash and Cattermole delight to paint but few of which now remain.

The Throne (OPPOSITE), *with chairs of State for the Prince Consort and Prince of Wales, and surmounted by its canopy, is the decorative climax of the Palace.*
The wood engraving (ABOVE) *is from* The Illustrated London News *of 1847*

1847,' wrote J. Cotton on January 15 that year. Apart from more than two miles (3.2 kilometres) of beam casings, the ceiling contains some 400 emblems, bosses and rosettes, and 900 feet (274 metres) of pierced inscriptions, endlessly repeating 'Dieu et mon droit'. This fretwork allows air to pass into the roof space: an integral feature of the hotly disputed ventilation system.

THE THRONE

The throne and canopy in the House of Lords are the decorative focus of the entire building. *The Illustrated London News* spoke rapturously of 'the golden glories of this exquisite marvel of art', whose ornament fulfilled every Gothic Revival expectation in terms of 'intricacy, variety and appropriateness'.

The steps to Queen Victoria's throne, flanked by chairs of State for the Prince Consort and Prince of Wales, are covered in a bright scarlet carpet 'of the richest velvet pile' decorated with a pattern of lions and roses. The wall behind the throne is decorated with the *lions passant* of England, carved and gilded on a red ground. Above them, surrounded by

Everywhere, and particularly in the library, oak sets the keynote. The present tone of the wood is probably lighter than Pugin would have had it; the only place where the original red-brown colour, which gives a more sumptuous effect, survives is the Chamber of the House of Lords and the Prince's Chamber.

THE WINDOWS

In the course of time, the twelve windows of the Lords' Chamber were filled with the glowing colours of stained glass, depicting the kings and queens of England (both 'Consort and Regnant', noted *The Illustrated London News* fussily). There was to be stained glass throughout the building. Little of it now remains: that in the House of Lords, the apogee of the scheme, was destroyed during the Blitz. While it was in place, the splashes of ruby red and ultramarine that fell from the windows on to the benches of the Lords must have made a fine sight. After the Second World War, Carl Edwards designed the present heraldic scheme of glass, in watery colours.

At the turn of the century, the text accompanying *Sir Benjamin Stone's Pictures* of the Houses of Parliament evokes the mood of the Chamber, much as Barry and Pugin must have intended:

 The solemn stillness and the soft light of a sacred edifice prevail. The figures of the Kings and Queens of England in their lofty stained glass windows look like saints in their antique garments. On pedestals, between the windows, are large bronze statues of knights, telling of times when the battle of principle was fought, not with the subtle mind and ready tongue of men in frock coats and silk hats, but with sword and battle-axe by soldiers in armour on prancing steeds. These are the bold and – many of them – wicked Barons who wrested Magna Carta from King John. In the subdued light of the House of Lords they seem like patriarchs and apostles.

By the time of Stone's book, much of the glass in the Palace, though not in the Chamber itself, had been remade to Pugin's designs, but without the original richness of colour. The figures were reproduced in *grisaille*, with almost clear glass being used in the background. This glass was blown out during the Second World War, to be replaced in the 1950s by heraldic glass in somewhat discordant colours. The effect of the *grisaille* glass has a beauty of its own, as can be seen from windows elsewhere in the Palace: for example the exquisite figures of Edward the Confessor, who established the Palace, and Queen Victoria, who rebuilt it, in the Norman Porch. Just one light survives to give a taste of the original House of Lords glass: the figure of William I, now in the peers' dining room. It was found in the old glass workshop a number of years ago; presumably it was a trial panel that had never been erected.

THE FURNITURE

When the furniture on the Lords' side of the Palace of Westminster was first surveyed in the early 1970s, it was discovered to comprise as many as 1,100 original pieces, which belonged to 300 different functional types. Some are relatively humdrum, some richly carved. Naturally, the grandest of all is the throne in the House of Lords' Chamber: a sunburst of gold – far too brightly lit, alas, under present conditions – that forms the decorative focus of the whole Palace of Westminster (see page 83). Most of the furniture is of oak, one of the more elaborate examples being the clerks' table in the centre of the Chamber, with its chairs for three bewigged clerks. The twelve legs take the form of pillars: rather surprisingly, the whole effect was intended, in plan, to recall the

One of the four rooms of the Lords' Library

portcullis that is the Westminster emblem. Presumably this pattern was inlaid into the leather top of the table, as well as being represented by the stretchers. Since the pattern has now disappeared, much of the point of the conceit has been lost. By contrast with the mixed success of this piece (obscured, during public opening hours, by disfiguring metal screens), the tables in the Prince's Chamber (originally called the Victoria Lobby) are glorious. They have octagonal tops, a form for which Pugin had a particular fondness. The under-carriage is a marvellous mixture of strength and plasticity, with arched braces reinforcing legs that are joined by ribbon-like ogee arches; each of the cross bars connecting the legs ends in a carved griffin.

The ubiquity of Pugin's designs gives the whole of House of Lords an unusual harmony. He designed quantities of metalwork, from the great brass gates that lead into the Chamber to the fingerplates on the oak doors, each of which is different. The gates are in brass: not a medieval material but one that Pugin seems specially to have liked. There are even brass inlays in some of the floors, adding further richness to the patterning of Minton's encaustic tiles. The tiles themselves demonstrate the revival of a medieval technique. This could hardly be said of the wallpaper, though Pugin took full advantage of the opportunities they gave for the display of flat pattern and rich, unbroken colour – a superb example of medieval principles being adapted to thoroughly nineteenth-century ends.

TELLING THE NATIONAL STORY

Barry's responsibility for the enrichment of his building was not total. It stopped short of works of art that could not be considered part of the architecture. No doubt this was a source of some annoyance to him: the Palace of Westminster is that relatively rare thing in British architecture – a building in which virtually every aspect of the interior, down to the clock faces, was specially commissioned for the purpose. Equally, Barry's determination to keep control over his vision, in the face of interference from his parliamentary clients, can have done little to endear him to those people entitled to have a say in the work. Prominent among the latter was Prince Albert. Married to Queen Victoria in 1840, he was, the very next year, made chairman of the Fine Arts Commission appointed by Parliament to mastermind the art content of its Palace.

In the centuries preceding the fire, many of the medieval glories of the Palace of Westminster had been lost to view. The nadir was reached in the 1800s when James Wyatt instructed workmen to hack away some recently discovered wall paintings in St Stephen's Chapel. Originally, however, the Palace of Westminster had been the principal residence of

A stained glass panel of William the Conqueror, now in the peers' dining room – the only one of the richly coloured kings and queens that originally adorned the Lords' Chamber to survive

Westminster Hall during the Coronation, 23 April 1685, 'with the manner of serving up the First Course of Hot Meat to their Majesties' Table'

the English kings, the decoration of which reflected their own sense of prestige. Westminster Hall was the largest structure of its kind in Europe; St Stephen's Chapel was Britain's answer to the richly painted Sainte Chapelle in Paris. It was in the spirit of this tradition that the Fine Arts Commission set about their deliberations. Something of their approach was already implicit in the architecture, with its series of State apartments, forming a grand ceremonial route that would be used only once a year at the State Opening of Parliament.

Barry had conceived his building partly as a kind of three-dimensional picture book of national history, showing particularly the kings and queens. The Fine Arts Commission followed exactly the same idea for the interior. They envisaged the works of art in the Palace as a series of *tableaux vivants* of defining moments in the national story – moments that, furthermore, exemplified some uplifting moral virtue. And they wanted these works of art to encourage the fine arts and to demonstrate just what British artistic talent was capable of. It was the attitude that would animate Prince Albert's later project, the Great Exhibition of 1851.

In the scale of artistic enrichment, the Lords weighed more heavily than the Commons – to the extent that, given the slow progress made in completing the works of art, the Commons received very few. Indeed, the Lords' Chamber, where work began, is one of the few spaces blessed with its full complement, including six frescoes (a cycle of three repeated at either end of the Chamber) showing at the north end Religion, Justice and Chivalry, and at the south end historical events illustrating these concepts. William Dyce's 'The Baptism of King Ethelbert', above the throne, was the first work of art to be completed.

THE NOBLE ART

The choice of both fresco as a medium and Dyce as an artist was significant. The Fine Arts Commission judged fresco to be the noblest form of painting, as well as the most permanent. This reflected the heroic vision of the whole enterprise, inspired by high ideals and intended to endure through the ages. Dyce, from Aberdeen, happened to be director of the Government School of Design but, more to the purpose, he was one of the few British painters with any experience of fresco. Not that much experience, unfortunately. The shortage of practical knowledge about fresco was to prove fatal to the Commission's hopes of longevity. A medium that was developed in the sunshine of pre-industrial Italy turned out to be hopelessly unsuitable for a gas-lit building beside the nineteenth-century Thames. Still, Dyce's works bore up better than others. More was painted in true fresco, pigment being directly applied on to damp plaster, and less as overpainting, adding extra detail on top of the stained plaster. In later years, it was the overpainting that suffered the worst degradation.

The historical cycle begins in the Royal Robing Room, where Dyce embarked on a series of seven frescoes on Arthurian themes. He had personally proposed the subject to Prince Albert, whose Germanic background predisposed him towards legend. Here, however, it was present not so much as legend, but as early history. The Arthurian court was one of the few medieval courts of which the Victorians could approve. Arthur was the first of our national heroes. Dyce chose his subjects to illustrate particular virtues such as Courtesy, Mercy, Religion (of course), Generosity and so on. The labour of painting them was immense, and not helped by the interruptions of workmen wanting to instal panelling and other elements of the architecture. He insisted on having the room to himself for three years, so that even the Queen was prevented from robing in it for the State Opening of Parliament. Even so, he died in 1864, with two of the cycle yet to complete.

Part of the trouble had been the costume adopted for the figures. Needless to say, this had been researched – or in the absence of much evidence, considered – in some depth, and it had been decided that chain mail was the appropriate dress. All the links took an excessively long time to paint in fresco. Dyce made the fatal decision to hasten the work by brushing in some of the detail when the plaster was dry. It soon started to flake off. Below Dyce's frescoes is a series of wooden reliefs

The Spirit of Chivalry *by Daniel Maclise, 1847, in the Lords' Chamber.*
The courtly values of chivalry are a central theme of the decoration

Religion: The Vision of Sir Galahad and his Company, *by William Dyce, 1851*
This fresco, depicting the prime knightly virtue of religion, was the first fresco in the Robing Room to be finished

by H.H. Armstead, showing the story of Arthur in chronological sequence. The delay caused by Dyce's monopoly of the room as he painted meant that Barry himself had died before the architectural decoration was finished; it was completed by Barry's second son, Edward Middleton.

The theme of the Royal Gallery is the English people in battle. Here, the choice of artist fell on Daniel Maclise. Eighteen panels were to have been painted with scenes of arms, from Boadicea onwards, but Maclise was only able to finish two enormous works showing 'The Death of Nelson' and 'The Meeting of Wellington and Blucher after Waterloo'. He very nearly gave up. The problem of how to paint elaborate compositions on walls strongly dappled by light from what was then Pugin's original stained glass could be solved: Prince Albert had the stained glass removed. But matching up each day's patch with the next – specially difficult, since the colour faded as it dried – defeated him. The solution, again promoted by Albert, was to study the technique variously known as waterglass, stereochrome or isinglass, developed by a group of Munich painters known as the Nazarenes. The artist painted on to dry plaster, his work then being coated with a layer of silicon which bonded permanently with the wall. It was an experimental technique, and it failed. Maclise's vivid colour quickly faded to a shadowy monochrome. Nobody understands the chemical process that caused the degradation; nobody can restore it, not least because of later attempts to revive the colours by impregnating the plaster with wax. Around the walls stand gilded carvings of mostly warrior kings and queens: as statues, more remarkable for valorous sentiment than artistic refinement.

Originally there was to have been a parade of marble statues in the Royal Gallery, culminating in the large seated statue of Queen Victoria, flanked by figures of Justice and Mercy, in the Prince's Chamber. The few statues that were finished are now in the Law Courts on the Strand. Queen Victoria is the only one currently in place. Or rather, out of place. All the rest of this room had been conceived as a romance on the Tudor and Stewart theme.

The tone is set by the series of portraits of sixteenth-century royal figures against gilded backgrounds: this is an astonishingly successful ensemble, when seen, as their elevated positions means they must be, from a distance, considering that they were executed by students from the Royal School of Art in South Kensington. Oak that is the colour of old, well-polished brogues gives a mellow note to the whole. On top of this rich stew the white marble sits like an inappropriate meringue. It is the work of John Gibson, a pupil of Canova, and attracted much praise while being carved in his studio in Rome.

Barry died in 1860, Albert the year after. They may sometimes have been a trial to each other, but after their deaths the energy went out of the project. The architecture was completed by Barry's son, Edward, in a more polychrome manner. The idea of enriching the building with works of art did not die: indeed it continues today. It has always been a cause dear to the heart of the Lords. The frescoes in St Stephen's Hall, the shared public entrance to both Houses, that represent a valiant, if artistically execrable, attempt to revive the spirit of the Mid-Victorians, were funded by individual peers. By that date, of course, the Commons had defeated the Lords in their centuries-long struggle for power; but their lordships still assumed an inherent superiority in matters of art and taste. Perhaps they still do.

Painting by Joseph Nash showing Queen Victoria at the State Opening of Parliament on 3 December 1857

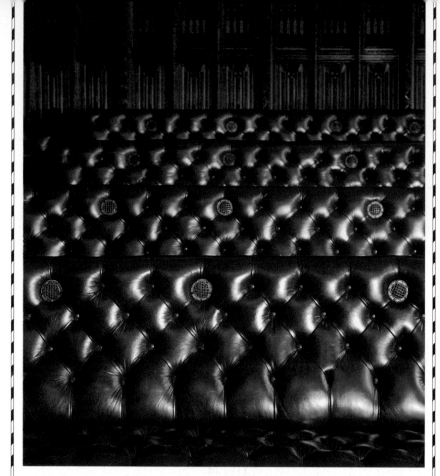

Detail of benches in the Chamber: red has been the House of Lords' colour since the sixteenth century. The brass portholes conceal speakers

THEIR LORDSHIPS SPEAK OUT

It is easy to see why the Victorians using the Chamber found it more appropriate to the pageant of State occasions than to the ordinary business of the House. In particular, there were complaints that peers could not make themselves heard. In those days, when fewer peers attended than today, addressing the expanses of empty red leather benches must have been dispiriting. Later legislators have come to appreciate the original superfluity of space, since the House is now almost ridiculously full. During Questions, even on an ordinary day, every available inch of bench and woolsack that can be perched upon is generally occupied.

The difficulties over voice projection have been solved by one of the most sophisticated sound systems in the world. Above the benches, little black microphones, suspended from wires, hover like a mass of dragonflies. Speakers have been ingeniously incorporated into the benches, as little brass portholes decorated with a portcullis grille. Between every microphone and every loudspeaker there is a fractionally different time delay, so that the real voice of the speaker arrives on the ear at exactly the same instant as the amplified one. The system was devised by the BBC, which has been televizing the Lords since 1985.

MAINTAINING THE PALACE

How does the man responsible for maintaining the Palace of Westminster today view Barry and Pugin's masterpiece? 'Detail, detail, detail,' says Henry Webber, the Director of Works: 'everywhere.' We are walking along one of the committee-room corridors, and he is pointing out loose frets in Gothic doors and incorrect brass handles. Only when every detail is perfect will his job be complete.

But with so big a building, it never will be. Besides, there are always new demands being made of it. The fires that devastated Hampton Court Palace and Windsor Castle made the authorities at Westminster sit up. Could it happen to us? they asked. They found that, all too easily, it could. Dr Reid's ventilation system left flues running throughout the building – just the sort of spaces that allow fire to spread rapidly. A fire safety officer was appointed to the Houses of Parliament, and he began a programme of installing fire detection equipment and fire barriers, some behind the scenes but some all too visible as fire doors. To the owners of many historic buildings, 'fire doors' are two of the most dread words in the language. They tend to be ugly, intrusive and inconvenient; often they destroy the character of the building they are intended to protect. At Westminster, a different approach has been taken, which should set the standard for the treatment of Grade 1 listed buildings. There are no obtrusive new fire doors; instead, Pugin's doors have been taken down, the linenfold panels carefully split in half and the doors rebuilt with intumescent paper in the middle. When they are put back, it is impossible to see the difference. Firedoors, but not as most people know them.

This approach is typical of the love now expended upon the Palace. Thanks to the enthusiasm of the late Sir Robin Cooke and others, Barry and Pugin's masterpiece recovered from the dark days of anti-Victorianism relatively early. There was a campaign to remake missing carpets and wallpapers, to Pugin's designs, in the 1970s; and work has continued on the detail, detail, detail ever since. During the Second World War, ceilings were painted white, presumably to save energy on lighting. These are now being grained. All the exposed woodwork in the Palace is quarter-sawn – that is, the planks are taken from the tree trunk at a different angle from usual – this gives the grain a distinctive broken pattern, somewhat like the skin of a mackerel. The grainer, using paint, has to imitate this effect.

One of the two elaborately carved doors in the Chamber used in divisions, with its brass grille. Each of the brass grilles on the doors throughout the House of Lords is to a different design

A heraldic lion on the Victoria Tower renewed in the 20th century as part of a programme to replace the decayed stonework of the Palace

Michael Heseltine was Environment Secretary, has been completed on most of the facades seen by the public (it continues in the internal courtyards). Almost all the original sculpture, badly eroded by the sulphurous air of old London, has been replaced. Decay is not a problem inside the building, but there are still acres of exposed stonework that have become grimy over the years. They raise a philosophical problem: should the grubbiness be regarded as patina, or something that ought to be cleaned off? Traditional methods of washing remove everything, leaving a surface that looks bald. Recently, however, experiments have been made with a revolutionary technique of cleaning with a laser. A tiny spot of light, about the diameter of a pencil, is worked over the surface of the stone, removing any obvious stains and disfigurements, while leaving the underlying tone undisturbed. The object is the reverse of soap-powder advertisements: not a wash that washes whiter, but a clean that does not look cleaned. It works. And the benefits are not just aesthetic: it is unnecessary to erect elaborate scaffolding or to take precautions against water-damage, and the work can be done piecemeal over weekends. This makes the method, though expensive, cost-effective, given the constraints of the Palace.

Wheelchair ramps, telephones – these must also be accommodated without disrupting the atmosphere of the Palace. There are already lifts, but whenever one of them needs to be modernized, the steel cage is replaced by one lined with wooden panelling. The peers, rightly, have high expectations of both the appearance and operation of their building. What are they most agitated by? Mr Webber has no hesitation: 'Air-conditioning, or the lack of it. Sun streams into the committee rooms overlooking the Thames, in the summer, and they are draughty in winter.' Meanwhile, the process of ornamenting the building continues, with new stained glass being fitted next to the hall keeper's lodge and a new organ being built for the undercroft chapel. H.R. Johnson of Stoke-on-Trent are reviving the encaustic process for making floor tiles, the Pugin originals having lost their pattern beneath the rubbing of feet. Recently the Lords' First World War memorial, a large bronze structure that originally stood in the oriel between Richard I and Edward III in the Royal Gallery, was found in an English Heritage store. 'Nobody knows how it got lost,' says Mr Webber. 'We are going to re-erect it in Black Rod's garden.'

Even parts of the building that cannot generally be seen receive their share of reverence. Recently, repairs to the roof over the Royal Gallery in the House of Lords have been under way: no easy task, given Barry's apparently eccentric choice of cast-iron plates. Each of the plates is 3 feet (1 metre) square, and weighs over a hundredweight (50 kilograms). This massive weight is supported on cast-iron trusses (cast iron being a fireproof material). The plates have not been completely impractical. 'They have lasted 150 years, and the leaks have not been that desperate,' says Mr Webber. But leaks there have been, at an increasing rate, due to the big thermal movement of the iron. However, it was decided to retain the plates, every one being marked, removed, cleaned with shot blasting, regalvanized, repainted and replaced. Spaces between the plates have been sealed with silicon mastic. The job has not been made easier by security demands and the need to stop working when the Lords is sitting.

Externally, the latest programme of stone-cleaning, begun when

The panelling in the Lords' Chamber is enriched with small busts of the kings of England. 'The busts of the very earliest Kings are, of course, imaginary,' wrote The Illustrated London News *in 1847, 'but those for which authorities could be found, are perfect specimens of portrait carving in wood, so truly is the resemblance between them and the originals.'*

THE NORMAN PORCH

ABOVE: *A corner of the Royal Gallery looking through to the Norman Porch*

OPPOSITE: *The soaring vaults of the Norman Porch create a cathedral-like effect.*
It was named after intended statues of the Norman sovereigns

PAGE 96: *William Pitt, first Earl of Chatham (1708-1778), Prime Minister 1766-68: a*
bust in the Norman Porch by Joseph Wilton, after 1780

PAGE 97: *The Norman Porch, with busts of noble Prime Ministers and a window showing*
Queen Victoria, in whose reign the present Palace of Westminster was built.

THE CHAMBER

ABOVE: *The Throne, with, behind it, the Cloth of Estate, symbolizing the monarch. Despite its name, The Cloth of Estate is made of carved wood, largely covered in 24-carat gold leaf*

OPPOSITE: *A view of the Chamber from the Bar, looking towards the Throne*

ABOVE: *A carved heraldic lion surveys the Chamber*

OPPOSITE: *The Strangers' Gallery at the Bar end of the Chamber, showing*
(above left) Maclise's The Spirit of Justice

ABOVE: *These angels kneeling beneath the Strangers' Gallery at the Bar end of the Chamber, exhibit some of the most beautiful carving in the House of Lords*

OPPOSITE: *One of the carved angels between the windows of the Chamber, beneath the Magna Carta barons*

ABOVE RIGHT: *The Press Gallery in the Chamber, with its seat for the doorkeeper*

RIGHT: *A corner of the Chamber, showing carved panelling, heads of kings and painted coats-of-arms*

OPPOSITE: *One of the vigorously carved royal beasts adorning the bench ends in the Chamber*

OPPOSITE: *Paul Hayter, one of the Clerks, sitting at the Clerk's Table in the Chamber*

BELOW: *On the Clerk's Table: the division hour glass, for timing votes, and a despatch box*

THE PRINCE'S CHAMBER

ABOVE: *John Gibson's statue of Queen Victoria*

RIGHT: *The sixteenth-century portraits in the Prince's Chamber were executed by Richard Burchett with the help of his pupils at the Royal School of Art, South Kensington*

RIGHT: Raleigh spreading his cloak as a carpet for Queen Elizabeth I, *a bronze relief panel by William Theed, 1855*

BELOW: *Detail of the ceiling in the Prince's Chamber*

OPPOSITE: *Another set of doors showing Pugin's superb metalwork. Note the hinges that allow the brass screens to be moved for cleaning the glass*

BELOW: *Some of the chairs designed by Pugin and made by Webb*

THE QUEEN'S ROBING ROOM

OPPOSITE: *The Queen's Robing Room.*
This is where the Queen puts on her crown before the State Opening of
Parliament. The Throne was presumably designed by E.M. Barry and
probably supplied by F. and J.G. Crace

ABOVE: *The stained glass shows a design by John Hardman Powell (Pugin's*
son-in-law) in grisaille

RIGHT: *A detail from the Robing Room doors.*

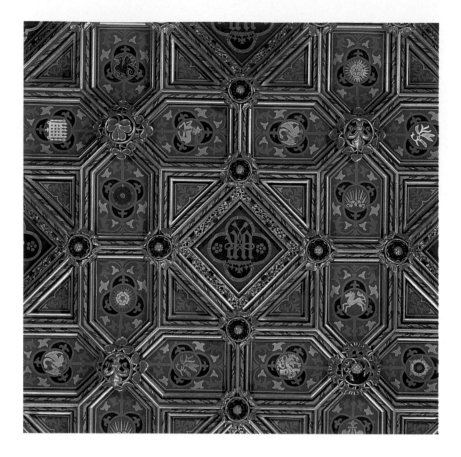

ABOVE: *The kaleidoscopic ceiling, decorated by Crace.*

RIGHT: *The frescoes by William Dyce illustrate the Arthurian legend, as do the carved panels by H.H. Armstead below them*

The Vision of Sir Galahad RELIGION and his Company

King Arthur UNKNOWN GENEROSITY spared by Sir Launcelot

THE ROYAL GALLERY

ABOVE: *Arch above the door between the Royal Gallery and the Robing Room*

OPPOSITE: *The doorway from the Royal Gallery into the Norman Porch. The gilded statues of William III and Queen Anne, as those of the other monarchs in the Royal Gallery, are by the justly forgotten Birnie Philips and do not live up to the rest of the decorative scheme*

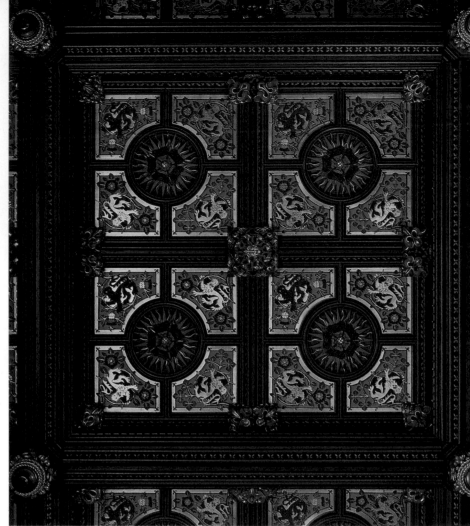

PAGES 118-9: *The Royal Gallery provides a grand processional route between the Robing Room and the Chamber. It was to have been decorated completely with frescoes, but the effort of finishing just the two great battle scenes* The Death of Nelson *and* The Meeting of Wellington and Blücher after Waterloo *defeated the artist Daniel Maclise*

ABOVE LEFT: *Figure of Justice by John Gibson, part of a group with Queen Victoria and Mercy, glimpsed through the sumptuously decorated doorway from the Royal Gallery*

ABOVE: *Ceiling of the Royal Gallery, with heraldic designs by Pugin*

LEFT: *Detail of the benches and carved panelling which line the Royal Gallery*

ABOVE: *Royal Gallery showing post-Second World War reproductions of Pugin's designs for heraldry of English and Scottish monarchs*

RIGHT: *One of the brass hinges on the door leading from the Royal Gallery to the Robing Room*

BELOW: *Encaustic floor tiles designed by Pugin and made by Minton, based on medieval examples*

THE LORDS' LIBRARY

ABOVE: *The Duke of Abercorn seated in the Lords' Library*

OPPOSITE: *Bookcases in the Library: note the ever-present armorial bearings above*

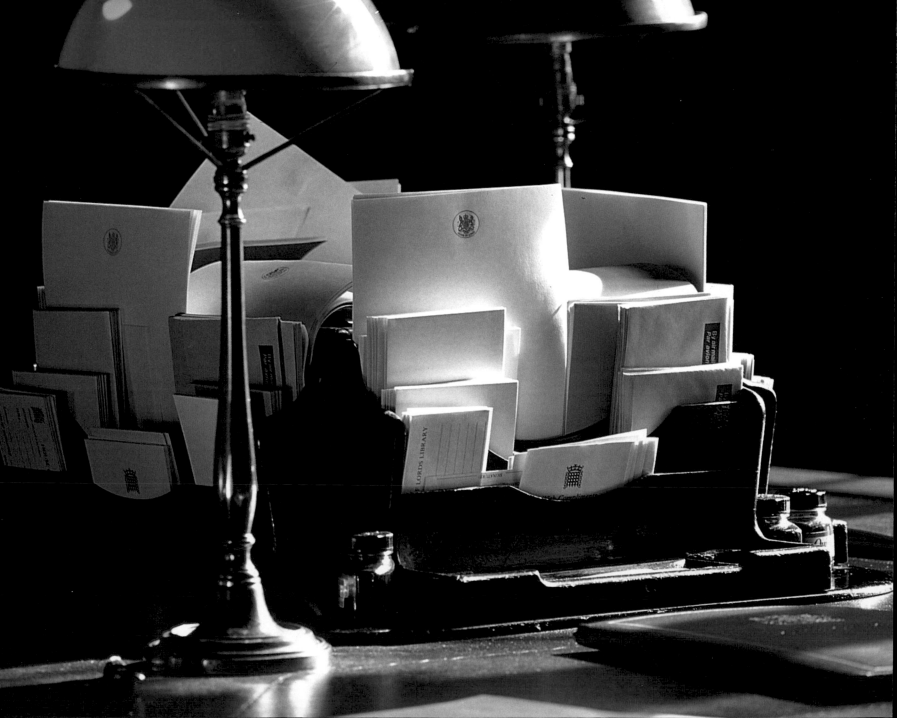

PAGES 124-5: *The Lords' Library*

OPPOSITE: *Library desk showing the House of Lords stationery;
below is a supply of nibs for dip pens*

ABOVE: *One of the beautiful clocks in the Lords' Library*

LEFT: *Detail of firedog in the Lords' Library*

Hood of Avalon
'92
iral

Horatio·Earl·Kitchener
1898
Field Marshal

Francis·Lord·Grenfell
1902
Field Marshal

John·Lord·Fisher
1909
Admiral·of·the·Fleet

William·Lord·Nicholson
1912
Field Marshal

ON TOP OF THE VICTORIA TOWER

LEFT: *Looking towards Big Ben and the City of London*

BELOW: *Some of the detail that only God normally sees*

OPPOSITE: *Room beneath the flagpole*

PAGE 128: *The main staircase, leading to the principal floor, impresses peers and visitors alike with the antiquity of the institution*

PAGE 129: *A door at the top of the main staircase, surrounded by coats-of-arms of Admirals and Field Marshalls*

LEFT: *A crown surmounting one of the four pinnacles at the top of the Victoria Tower*

BELOW: *One of the turrets at the top of the Victoria Tower*

OPPOSITE RIGHT: *Detail of one of the turrets, showing heraldic lions*

OPPOSITE LEFT: *Detail of a door surround in the Royal Gallery*

A BRIEF HISTORY: WATCHED OVER BY ANGELS

One might have expected the decorative scheme of the House of Lords to dwell on the history of the Lords itself; but as we have seen, it concentrated instead on the history of England. Fortunately, there was already a symbol of the institution's longevity in the form of Westminster Hall, and by a miracle it escaped the fire of 1834. Today Westminster Hall is one of the spaces, like St Stephen's Hall and the undercroft chapel that lies below it, whose use is shared between the Commons and the Lords. It has longer associations with the Lords than with the other House, since the Commons did not exist when it was built. The Lord Great Chamberlain, as the representative of the Queen, is consulted about decisions concerning its maintenance.

It suited the Victorians to think that Edward the Confessor had founded the Palace of Westminster. He was, after all, a saint and as an Anglo-Saxon more obviously English than the Norman kings. In the middle of the eleventh century he began rebuilding the abbey church of St Peter, better known as Westminster Abbey, which lay in an unpromising location outside the walls of London. Nothing can now be seen of it. Westminster Hall, by contrast, owes its present dimensions to the altogether less saintly figure of William Rufus, William the Conqueror's second son and his successor. Building began in the late decades of the eleventh century, and in 1099 William Rufus came over from France and held court in his new hall for the first time.

THE FIRST SEAT OF PARLIAMENT

Westminster Hall must have astonished contemporaries through its sheer size, being 240 feet (73 metres) long and 67 feet 6 inches (20.5 metres) wide. This is the size of the present hall, whose outer walls, below the stringcourse, contain the original masonry behind later

Gilded angels on the Throne, gracefully supporting the royal arms

refacings. There was no other hall on this scale in England, and probably none in Europe, when it was built. Its general appearance would have been different from the present hall. There was no hammerbeam roof: this was added by Richard II. The Norman masons were not able to create a roof of this span without the support of aisles, which divided the internal space. Light came from an arcaded gallery of round-headed windows that probably ran round four sides. Outside, the columns of the aisle were matched by buttresses to help take the thrust of the roof. Such a building would have seemed an awe-inspiring achievement to the abbots and archbishops, the earls, thanes and knights, that William Rufus entertained there.

Later chroniclers liked to portray William Rufus as dismissing Westminster Hall with megalomaniac insouciance as not nearly big enough. Those stories must be apocryphal: adduced to illustrate the folly of a generally bad king. In fact, the capabilities of the masons were stretched to construct this great building as it was. Evidence of this can be seen in a serious mistake they made in aligning the columns and buttresses. Those on the west side are 4 feet (1.2 metres) adrift from those on the east. The most likely explanation, suggested by Howard Colvin in *The History of the King's Works*, is that the Norman hall was built around an existing building that continued to function as work progressed. This would have made it difficult for the masons to take accurate measurements from one side to another. William Rufus was perhaps lucky to have a hall that, unlike so many other ambitious medieval structures, did not collapse.

It could not be said that the Norman kings really lived there. Like the Anglo-Saxon rulers, they were constantly on the move between their different possessions, as the needs of government and the enjoyment of hunting dictated. Westminster Hall was built to impress, and it would have been used for great ceremonial gatherings, at which the king sought to dazzle the great ones of the land. It is known that each year William Rufus's father, William the Conqueror, celebrated three feasts in England at which he wore his crown: at Easter in Winchester, at Christmas in Gloucester and at Whitsuntide in Westminster. William Rufus would have continued the practice.

There was as yet no fixed administrative centre for the kingdom, the seat of government being where the king happened to be at the time. At this date the principal administrative activity was the sending of the king's letters, which did not require much infrastructure. The only aspect of the court that could not be easily transported was the treasure, which remained at Winchester. It was not, however, Winchester that became the centre for the bureaucracy that expanded rapidly under later kings. The principal function of government was the exchequer, and that was established at Westminster. It developed its own treasury, which finally absorbed the Winchester one in the reign of King John. Though subsequent monarchs owned many royal manors and palaces, Westminster held pride of place until Henry VIII moved his court to the Palace of Whitehall, leaving Westminster to the administrators. Until then, every king had sought to do something to adorn this Palace that was a residence, a setting for state ceremony and the centre of civil administration.

Naturally the kings came to hold their councils more frequently at Westminster than elsewhere. These councils, which are the ancestors of Parliament (see the outline sketch of the history of the House of Lords on page 138), were sometimes occasions of drama. In 1229 Henry III's Council of prelates, nobles, knights and tenants-in-chief met at Westminster to resist the Pope's demand for a tithe of all movables in England and Ireland, which they conceded only after the threat of ex-communication had been made against them (even then Ranulph, Earl of Chester, would not submit). It was again at Westminster that, in 1252, Henry III solemnly swore, before his Council, to uphold Magna Carta and the Charter of Forests. Every man present held a lighted taper except, on the grounds that he was not a priest, the King. Then the tapers were thrown down on to the floor as the Archbishop prayed that the soul of anyone who broke the charters would be similarly extinguished. Theatre of this kind emphasized the importance of an event (not that it did any good in the case of Henry III: he obtained absolution from the oath and carried on as before). Lavish ceremonial that would be remembered and talked about helped reinforce whatever message the authorities wished to put out, in the age before many people could read. The same is true of the grisly deaths meted out to traitors and rebels. Sir William Wallace met a traditionally gruesome end after one of the many great state trials to be held in Westminster Hall. Westminster Hall was also the scene of Edward I's celebrated Model Parliament of 1295, once regarded as the first Parliament to include an element of the Commons, though this distinction actually falls to Parliaments earlier in Edward's reign.

THE REBUILDING OF WESTMINSTER HALL

To some monarchs, state ceremony assumed a beauty of its own, beyond its propaganda value. Richard II was addicted to it. It was in keeping with his taste for ritual, as well as art, that he should have rebuilt Westminster Hall. Such was the scale and durability of William Rufus's achievement that his hall remained virtually unaltered for 200 years. It had received various accretions, for the sake of the king's privacy and comfort and to house departments such as the Exchequer, the Court of Common Pleas and the King's Bench. Now, at the end of the fourteenth century, the hall itself was looking, to Richard II's sophisticated eye, distinctly old-fashioned, with its Romanesque detail and interior encumbered with columns. His first contribution was to commission a series of stone statues of kings, showing all the monarchs from Edward the Confessor until himself. Made by Thomas Canon, a marbler from Dorset, and painted by Nicholas Tryer, they were intended to stand in the hall, though for some reason only half a dozen were put in place. Those are there to this day. A certain provinciality in the carving only add to their *gravitas*. 'Gilding and vibrant colour would have been perhaps the most immediate and important aspects of the commission when they first stood in the hall,' writes Malcolm Hay in *Westminster Hall and the Medieval Kings*. 'Visitors would have been impressed by these larger-than-life figures, each wearing a tall, deeply carved and brightly-gilded crown and flowing emerald-green and crimson robes.' Tryer was paid not much less for decorating the statues than Canon was for carving them. Alas, their sumptuous pigmentation has long since disappeared.

THE HAMMERBEAM ROOF

The statues were but a modest prelude to the great work of rebuilding the roof. There is some reason to suppose that the weight of the old roof had finally come to push the walls outwards, making repairs necessary. The need for repair may have sown the idea of total replacement. But the new work went far, far beyond what was structurally necessary. It entailed nothing less than the construction of English medieval carpentry's grand masterpiece: not only, as Colvin notes, the largest hammerbeam roof in Northern Europe but, as far as we can tell, the

An early photograph of Westminster Hall, showing the hammerbeam roof

first. The master mason responsible for the stonework side of the project was Henry Yevele, then in his seventies. He was more than a craftsman, having supervised many great royal and other building projects over the previous two decades. John Harvey published a biography of Yevele in 1944, a time when national distinctiveness was particularly prized. In it he writes:

 The remarkable thing about Yevele, and it is the very kernel of his greatness, is that he did for our architecture what Chaucer did for our language, giving to it a special character which was altogether national, even though it was part of a common European heritage, like the other arts and sciences.

Yevele would certainly have known Chaucer, who was also in the King's employ at this time. Yevele heightened the walls, refaced them and built the heavy buttresses that would sustain the roof. He studded the whole with carved emblems belonging to Richard II and the Plantagenet kings. Towers were built to either side of the north doorway, which became a ceremonial entrance somewhat in the manner of a cathedral.

The roof itself was the work of Master Hugh Herland. Spanning so great a width was a prodigious achievement, which provided a large area of open floor below. The glory of it, however, resides not just in the structural accomplishment but in the design: tiers of hammerbeams are combined with lateral arched braces, creating a grand and satisfying rhythm, a note of mystery being added by the half-light through which it is all seen. We can follow the construction of the roof through the accounts. The timbers were shaped at a workshop near Farnham called The Frame. Hundreds of oak trees were brought thither from woods around London. Once the component parts of the roof had been carved, they were taken to the Thames by cart, and then to Westminster by river. The weight of the roof has been estimated at 660 tons, so the transport alone was quite a feat. Scaffolding to put it up was erected in 1395-96.

Even before the roof was finished, the hall was pressed into use for two royal events that took place in 1377: the coronation of Queen Isabella and the holding of a parliament. In later years, the great space provided by the hall was made to serve many purposes, some of the different functions taking place at the same time. The Courts of the King's Bench and of Chancery occupied different corners. The hall also served as a kind of market, with stallholders selling hats, spectacles, books and other wares. The bustle and noise are almost unimaginable to the modern visitor, confronted by a space as empty as it is vast and used as little more than a spacious corridor to connect one part of the Palace to another. The angels in the roof must wait for the one or two great state occasions that, in the course of a year, to see the Hall brought back to life.

THE HOUSE OF LORDS THROUGH THE CENTURIES

The history of the Lords as an institution is beyond the reach of this book, but the following is a brief resumé of its development.

ELEVENTH CENTURY

The origins of Parliament are generally traced back to the *witenagemot*, or assembly of wise men, with whom Anglo-Saxon kings would take counsel. The wise men included prelates, territorial magnates and the king's own ministers. After 1066, William I imposed the French feudal system, granting the brutal individuals who were closest to him enormous tracts of land over which they could hold sway, in return for military service. Some of them participated in the councils called by the king. Later documents refer to one of these councils, held in 1081, as a parliament. It cannot, however, be said to have much in common with later Parliaments, since its composition and status were ad hoc.

THIRTEENTH CENTURY

Assemblies of England's most powerful men were increasingly summoned to share their wisdom with the king. Their assistance was sought particularly in times of financial difficulty for the monarch. For the great barons who contributed most to the Exchequer this was not enough: they wanted to exert more influence over how their money was spent and how much of it had to be raised. To that end Simon de Montfort led a rebellion against Henry III, imprisoning him and, in 1265, summoning his own Parliament in the King's name. The coalition that de Montfort had established did not last long: de Montfort, who was the King's brother-in-law, seemed no better an option than the King and he was defeated and killed at the Battle of Evesham. But the idea of parliaments took hold. Henry III's son, Edward I, called parliaments which included representatives from the counties, cities and boroughs — otherwise known as the knights of the shires, citizens and burgesses.

FOURTEENTH CENTURY

The fourteenth century saw Parliament coalesce into two distinct houses. The process is succinctly described by Lord Longford in *A History of the House of Lords*:

 By 1332 the Lords and Commons were meeting in separate chambers. By 1363 the Commons had its own Clerk, a man called Robert de Melton from the Court of Chancery who was paid 100 shillings a year for life, plus any perks he could get; and

A fireplace in the Bishops' Robing Room: note the ecclesiastical firedogs

by 1377 the Commons was so entirely separate from the king and the Lords that it had its own Speaker — that is, the man who spoke to the king on their behalf and had the untrammelled right to do so. 'The Commons' it was certainly called by then, but not yet the 'House of Commons'.

But it was the king who still ruled. He tended to summon parliaments more often, but only when he had need of them, and principally to raise more taxes.

FIFTEENTH CENTURY

In the course of the fifteenth century, relations between the Commons and the Lords came to be codified, the Lords establishing themselves as the Upper or Higher House. By a process that is impossible to define, the Lords Temporal emerged as a body of men whose rights and titles came to them by inheritance. Previously, the king had chosen whomever he wished to attend Parliament. Now Parliament acquired its own independent identity, although it was still only summoned occasionally (this remained the case until the Glorious Revolution of 1688). The Lords Temporal called themselves peers, meaning that, whatever their different ranks of duke, marquess, earl, viscount and baron, they regarded themselves as equals within Parliament: a solid political mass. They were joined in the Upper House by the Lords Spiritual, a less regular body of bishops, abbots and priors.

SIXTEENTH CENTURY

The Tudors summoned parliaments when they needed them; when Henry VII was establishing himself, for example, and when Henry VIII wanted support for policies surrounding the Reformation and his divorce. But they were not inclined to summon them too often.

With the suppression of the monasteries in 1539, the composition of the Lords suffered an upheaval. Until then the Lords Spiritual consisted of bishops, abbots and priors. After 1539, only bishops attended and the Lords Temporal formed the majority for the first time. 'Within the space of a few months the aspect of the parliament chamber had been drastically altered,' wrote Enoch Powell and Keith Wallis in *The House of Lords in the Middle Ages*. The impact was all the greater given the small size of the House of Lords in comparison with modern times. Throughout the reign of Queen Elizabeth I, the number was never much more than 90, with a constant 26 bishops and a fluctuating number of Lords (at the highest 65, at the lowest 52). By the Queen's death, a third of the old nobility had disappeared through extinction or through being convicted for treason. These losses were not quite made good by new creations, and the House of Lords ended the reign as an even more select band, in terms of size, than it had been at the beginning.

SEVENTEENTH CENTURY

James I showed no scruples in the creation of new peers, whether to reward his epicene friends or to raise money. He revised the ceremony of introduction to avoid the necessity of having to be present himself. 'The frequent Promotions to Titles of Honour and Dignity since King James came to the Crown of England took off from the respect due to nobility,' lamented a scandalized Garter King of Arms, Sir Edward Walker, in the 1650s. 'The Curtain being drawn, they were discovered to be men that heretofore were reverenced as angels.'

During the Civil War, probably about half the House of Lords supported the King, a quarter threw in their lot with the Parliamentarians and the remaining quarter did their best not to take sides. In 1642 the bishops were excluded from the House of Lords. After the King's defeat, the Lords refused to pass an ordinance for his trial and the House was abolished. Cromwell reinstated a House of Lords, of a sort, in the 1650s, though appointed entirely by nomination – as it could be again as a result of the present reform proposals. Several of the first Cromwellian peers were related to the Lord Protector. After the Restoration the House of Lords resumed sitting in its pre-Cromwell guise, the bishops returning with the Clergy Act of 1661.

The Lords more than regained its old confidence, not from its actions as a House but from the positions occupied and honours worn by individual peers. The family estates that had been confiscated were returned. But the Lords was not always able to assert the authority it would have wished. Resolutions passed in 1671 and 1678 put the pre-eminence of the Commons in financial matters on an official basis after attempts by the Lords to breach the convention.

In 1688 King James II fled England, throwing the Great Seal, the symbol of the authority of the Crown, into the Thames. One result of the Glorious Revolution, which brought over William of Orange and his wife Mary as King and Queen, would be the Bill of Rights of 1689, which established the authority of Parliament over the King. Nevertheless, the people who had principally been responsible for effecting the revolution had largely been noblemen: representatives of the old hierarchy dedicated to settling a new order.

EIGHTEENTH CENTURY

Before the fire that destroyed the old Houses of Parliament, giving Barry the opportunity to create the icon of democracy which is the present building, the importance of the House of Lords lay in the people attending it, rather than the institution seated at Westminster.

 The significance of the House of Lords in the eighteenth century lies not so much in the corporate power as in the

A handsomely engraved ticket allowing entrance to Westminster Hall for George IV's Coronation in 1821. This one is for Viscount Exmouth

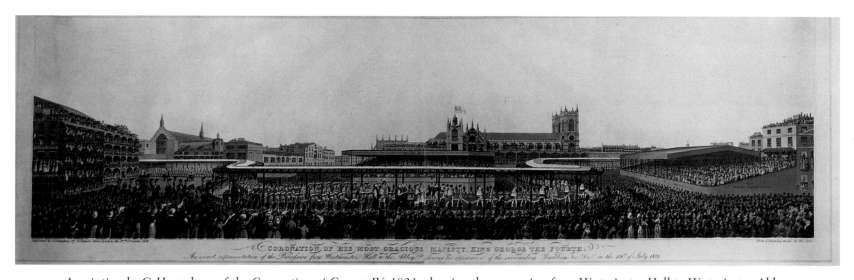

A painting by G Humphrey of the Coronation of George IV, 1821, showing the procession from Westminster Hall to Westminster Abbey

Joseph Nash's watercolour of Queen Victoria in a Chamber entirely filled
with women. The explanation of this event remains a mystery

An early print showing the entrance to the House of Lords

House of Lords in the Age of Reform, 1784-1837: 'No other single individual has exercised so great an influence as he upon the personnel of the Chamber. Within the space of his first Administration the membership of the House increased by as much as 40 per cent.' Like others before and after him, he used the grant of peerages both as a reward for past support and to bolster his position in the Lords. As Disraeli wrote memorably in *Sybil*: 'He created a plebeian aristocracy and blended it with the patrician oligarchy. He made peers of second-rate squires and fat graziers. He caught them in the alleys of Lombard Street, and clutched them from the counting-houses of Cornhill.' Pitt died in 1806, but his example was followed by his successors. Between 1783 and 1837 the House of Lords nearly doubled in size, from 238 members to 433.

The century ended with one of the most controversial legal processes ever witnessed in the Lords, the impeachment of Warren Hastings, Governor-General of the East India Company, for corruption. When it opened in 1788, the trial attracted enormous interest, and Westminster Hall was thronged both with peers and spectators. There followed some of the greatest orations ever heard in Parliament. But the proceedings dragged on for seven years, and by the end of it hardly any peers felt themselves competent to vote. Hastings was acquitted on all charges, but the cost of fighting the case ruined him.

NINETEENTH CENTURY

1820 saw what was, in effect, another great trial when a Tory administration attempted to bring in a Bill of Pains and Penalties

personal influence of its members. The House of Lords was still important, but what made it so was less their lordships' deliberations at Westminster than their political and social activities on their estates. The governance of England was mainly in the hands of a titled oligarchy, a landowning aristocracy. The faded and drab solemnity of the old House of Lords in the ancient Palace of Westminster was but a dim reflection of the glories of Chatsworth and Clermont, Alnwick and Stowe, Woburn and Blenheim.

Thus A.S. Turbeville in his *The House of Lords in the XVIIIth Century*. After the fire, the position was more or less reversed: it became impossible to separate the function of the building from its physical character, and this has continued to colour the proceedings long after the political power of the great country estates has waned.

Three external events served to change the composition of the House of Lords. The first two were the Acts of Union (with Scotland in 1707 and with Ireland in 1800), which entitled Scottish and Irish peers to elect representatives from among their number to sit in the Lords. The third was the advent of William Pitt the Younger as Prime Minister in 1783. To quote Turbeville again, in the next of his three volumes, *The*

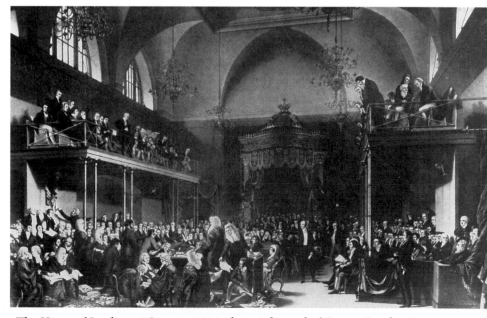

The House of Lords on 1 January 1820, during the trial of Queen Caroline for adultery, with temporary galleries by Soane

against Queen Caroline. This would have dissolved her marriage to George IV on grounds of adultery. The proceedings were so unpopular that Westminster Hall and the surrounding streets had to be heavily manned by soldiers, and the House of Lords found itself depicted as the bully of a defenceless woman. It helped establish an image of the Upper House as oppressors of the people, a role in which it would be in danger of being typecast during the agitation preceding the various Catholic Emancipation and Reform Bills over the coming two decades.

In the early nineteenth century, between a third and half of Members of Parliament were controlled by patronage, much of it located in the House of Lords. In 1831 *The Gentleman's Magazine* calculated that 96 peers secured the return of 190 members. So reform of the Commons, by abolishing rotten boroughs, giving more seats to large towns and extending the franchise, necessarily touched the Lords, where it was bitterly opposed. Opposition to reform was lead by the Duke of Wellington. However, the Prime Minister, Lord Grey, won the King's agreement that, if the Bill could not be passed in the Lords, he would create a sufficient number of new peers to assure a government majority.

Several diarists comment on the lassitude that characterized most Lords proceedings, but great constitutional measures could occasion a very high level of attendance. Nearly the whole peerage was present when, following a debate that lasted throughout the night, the Great Reform Bill was finally passed. That capitulation on the part of Tory peers prepared them for the experience of the Repeal of the Corn Laws in 1846. Led by the Duke of Wellington, the Tories in the House of Lords helped a measure that operated both against their landowning interests and their protectionist convictions. It was a retreat, one of many in the subsequent history of Conservatism in the Lords, but, as on other occasions, it prevented a constitutional stalemate with the Commons and kept the party together. 'God bless you, Duke,' was the cry of the little crowd who gathered as the peers emerged after the vote at 4.30 a.m. The Duke's reply did not suggest that he was overwhelmed by love of the populace. 'For heaven's sake, people, let me get to my horse,' he exclaimed.

But then the great Reform Act, though it reorganized the system and benefitted the middle classes, did not do much for democracy. The second Reform Act of 1867 included many working men in the franchise, inaugurating, it might have been thought, a political class that would not naturally follow the lead given by the aristocracy. Consequently it was, in its way, as much a milestone for the House of Lords as the previous Reform Act had been. The significant point is that, having been introduced by Benjamin Disraeli, as Chancellor of the Exchequer to Lord Derby, it was passed by the House of Lords without crisis. Another strategic withdrawal.

The Bishopric of Manchester Act 1847 (and later Acts) limited the number of bishops entitled to sit. Most of the Irish and all the Welsh bishops ceased to sit when their respective churches were disestablished in 1869 and 1920.

The Appellate Jurisdiction Act 1876 enabled the sovereign to create Lords of Appeal in Ordinary (Law Lords) to fulfil the judicial function of the House of Lords. They were, in effect, the first life peerages.

1894 saw the Lords reject Gladstone's second Home Rule Bill by a majority of over ten to one. 'With that rejection,' observes Gladstone's biographer Lord Jenkins, 'the hope of Anglo-Irish reconciliation within a common Britannic polity died.' It was the political struggles over the Irish question that left the Conservatives and Unionist party with the ascendancy in the House of Lords which is such an irritant to Labour.

TWENTIETH CENTURY

In 1909 the Lords rejected the Liberal Government's budget. The Liberals then introduced a Bill to end the Lords' power to reject legislation approved by the Commons, which was passed after a general election persuaded the King to threaten the creation of a large number of Liberal peers. The Parliament Act 1911 provided that:

- Money Bills approved by the Commons became law if not passed without amendment by the Lords within one month.
- Other Public Bills, except one to extend the life of a Parliament, became law without the consent of the Lords, if passed by the Commons in three successive sessions, providing that two years elapsed between Second Reading and final passing in the Commons.

In 1922 elections for Irish representative peers ceased. The Parliament Act 1949 reduced the delaying power of the 1911 Act, in respect of Public Bills other than Money Bills to two sessions and one year respectively. The Life Peerages Act 1958 (a Tory reform) permitted the creation of baronies for life, with no limit on numbers, to persons of either sex. At about the same time allowances for peers' out-of-pocket expenses and the system of 'leave of absence' for peers who did not wish to, or could not, attend the House for a longer period were introduced. The Peerage Act 1963 allowed hereditary peeresses to be members of the House, hereditary peerages to be disclaimed for life and for all Scottish peers to sit. In 1968 the Labour Government introduced the Parliament (No. 2) Bill, which would have created a two-tier House of members who could speak and vote and others who could speak but not vote. The Bill was so held up at committee stage in the House of Commons by both Labour and Conservative MPs that it had to be abandoned. 🞲

An angel roof boss and vaulting in the Norman Porch. The mosaic shows the rose of England

Facts, Figures and Faces

i. CELEBRATED STATE TRIALS AND IMPEACHMENTS TO HAVE BEEN HELD IN WESTMINSTER HALL

Sir William Wallace	1305
Perkin Warbeck	1498
Saint Thomas More and Saint John Fisher	1535
The Duke of Somerset, Protector	1551
Guy Fawkes	1606
The Earl of Stafford	1641
Charles 1	1649
The Seven Bishops	1688
Dr Sacheverell	1710
The Rebel Lords of the '15	1716
The Rebel Lords of the '45	1746-7
Warren Hastings	1788-95

ii. KEY EVENTS ON THE ROAD TO REFORM

Since reform of the House of Lords is now an issue, it is worth reviewing the other attempts to reform it that have been made, with varying degrees of success, during the course of the twentieth century. They are admirably described in the information sheet *House of Lords Reform 1850-1970* published by the House of Lords Information Office, from which the following is derived.

As the century opened, the powers of the Lords were equal to those of the Commons, except that the House of Lords recognized Common's privilege in financial matters. It retained the right to reject financial legislation altogether, but rarely exercised it. Then, as now, there was an overwhelming Conservative majority in the Lords, demonstrated in the massive defeat of Gladstone's second Home Rule Bill in 1893. This defeat excited the Liberals in the cause of reform.

The Parliament Act 1911

In 1907, when the Liberal Government was unable to enact some of its major proposals for lack of a majority in the House of Lords, Lord Newton, a Conservative peer, introduced a Bill which would have ended the automatic right of a hereditary peer to a seat in the House of Lords; the Bill was withdrawn and a select committee, chaired by the Earl of Rosebery, was appointed in lieu to consider proposals for reform.

When the committee reported in 1908, it echoed Lord Newton's Bill by concluding that 'it was undesirable that the possession of a peerage should of itself give the right to sit and vote in the House of Lords.'

In 1909 the House of Lords rejected Lloyd George's budget; the Liberal Government, returned in the ensuing election in 1910, laid before the House of Commons resolutions on the restriction of the powers of the House of Lords, which were later turned into the Parliament Bill. The House of Lords also approved a number of resolutions proposing reform, particularly of its composition, whilst asserting the necessity of 'a strong and efficient Second Chamber'; but a constitutional conference of Liberals and Unionists established in the same year failed to reach agreement on the powers a Second Chamber ought to have.

In 1911 the Marquess of Lansdowne, Leader of the Opposition in the Lords, introduced a Bill proposing a reconstituted House of Lords consisting mainly of indirectly elected members. However, the Bill was dropped when the Government pressed on with its own Parliament Bill. This dealt with powers only, but in its preamble expressed the need and intention to deal in the future with the composition of the Lords and with relations between the two Houses. The Bill was passed by the House of Lords in August 1911, under the threat of the creation of a large number of Liberal Peers to ensure its passage should the Bill be rejected.

The Parliament Act 1911 provided that a Bill certified by the Speaker as a Money Bill should receive Royal Assent and become an Act of Parliament without the consent of the House of Lords if it had not been passed by the Lords without amendment within one month of its being sent up from the House of Commons. The Act also provided that any other Public Bill, except one for extending the life of a Parliament, could become an Act of Parliament without the consent of the House of Lords if it had been passed by the House of Commons in three successive sessions, two years having elapsed between its first Second Reading and its final passing in the House of Commons.

The Bryce Report and other proposals 1912-1945

The 1911 Parliament Act was widely regarded as a temporary measure which should be either replaced or considerably improved. In 1917 a conference consisting of fifteen members of each House of Parliament and chaired by Viscount Bryce was appointed to consider both the composition and the powers of a reformed Second Chamber.

The majority of the conference recommended that the Second Chamber should consist of 246 members indirectly elected by MPs grouped into regional units, together with 81 members chosen by a Joint Standing Committee of both Houses. (All 81 were to be hereditary peers or bishops in the first instance; the number was then gradually to be reduced to 30 hereditary peers and bishops and 51 others.) The Law Lords were to sit ex officio. Except for those holding seats ex officio, all members would hold seats for twelve years, one third retiring every fourth year. The conference envisaged that the Second Chamber would have full powers over legislation that was not of a financial character, but would not be able to amend or reject purely financial legislation; a small Joint Standing Committee of both Houses would declare which Bills, or parts of Bills, were of this type. Any difference between the two Houses would be resolved by means of a 'Free Conference Committee' consisting of up to 30 members of each House. In certain circumstances a Bill that was agreed by the House of Commons and an adequate majority of the Free Conference might pass into law without the agreement of the Second Chamber.

The conference reported in 1918 at a time when the Government was preoccupied with the war and no action was taken to implement the Bryce Report. Though Lords reform was discussed throughout the 1920s and into the 1930s, no legislation was passed.

The Parliament Act 1949

In 1947 the Government, with a view to safeguarding its Bills in the fourth session of that Parliament, introduced a Parliament Bill in the House of Commons. This Bill dealt only with the powers of the House, and in response to pressure from both Conservatives and Liberals the debate on the Second Reading of the Bill in the Lords was adjourned while talks between the party leaders took place. The conference discussed both powers and composition, regarding the two as interdependent, but talks broke down in April 1948 over the period of delay that the House of Lords should be able to interpose in a Bill's progress. However, tentative agreement had been reached on certain principles regarding the role and composition of a reformed House. The more important of these were that a Second Chamber 'should be complementary to and not a rival to' the Lower House, that there should not be a permanent majority assured for any one political party, that heredity should not by itself constitute a qualification for admission to a reformed Second Chamber, and that women should be allowed to be appointed Lords of Parliament.

After the 1948 conference had broken down, the House of Lords rejected the Parliament Bill on Second Reading. The Bill was then passed into law in 1949 under the terms of the Parliament Act 1911 – only the third Bill to be passed in this way. The Parliament Act 1949 amends its predecessor of 1911 by reducing the number of sessions in which a Bill must be passed by the Commons from three to two, and reducing the period between the first Second Reading and the final passing in the Commons from two years to one.

The Life Peerages Act 1958

Harold Macmillan's Conservative Government initiated the Life Peerages Act 1958. This empowered the Crown to create life peers who would be entitled to sit and vote in the House of Lords and whose peerages would expire on their death. Life peerages could be conferred upon women.

The Peerage Act 1963

Although life peeresses were created under the Life Peerages Act, hereditary peeresses in their own right were still unable to sit in the House of Lords. By the Peerage Act 1963, initiated by the Macmillan Government, peeresses in their own right were admitted to the House, as were all Scottish peers. The Act also enabled disclaimers to be made for life or hereditary peerages.

The attempts at comprehensive reform by the Labour Government, 1967-69

The Labour election manifesto for 1966 pledged the party, if returned to power, to introduce legislation 'to safeguard measures approved by the House of Commons from frustration by delay or defeat in the House of Lords'; in the event, a Labour administration under Harold Wilson was returned with a majority of 99. The Queen's Speech for 1967-8 contained the following words:

 'Legislation will be introduced to reduce the powers of the House of Lords and to eliminate its present hereditary basis, thereby enabling it to develop within the framework of a modern Parliamentary system. My Government are prepared to enter into consultations appropriate to a constitutional change of such importance.'

Accordingly, inter-party talks on Lords' Reform took place at a conference between party leaders from 8 November 1967 to 20 June 1968, when the talks were broken off by the Government after the

Earl Grey appealing to the bishops to pass the Reform Bill on 1 January 1831. They voted against it on this occasion

peers to enable them to continue in active participation as voting members. It was proposed that the government of the day should have a small majority over the opposition parties, but, taking account of the non-aligned voting members, not an absolute majority of the whole House. The reformed House would be able to impose a delay of six months from the date of disagreement between the Houses on the passage of non-financial public legislation. After this delay a Bill could be submitted for Royal Assent by resolution of the House of Commons. The Lords would be able to require the House of Commons to reconsider subordinate legislation, but would not be able to reject it outright.

The White Paper was debated in both Houses. In the Lords, after a free-day debate in which opinion was generally favourable (despite some Conservative back-bench opposition), it was approved by 251 votes to 56. In the Commons the debate was much more critical of the Government's proposals. This was particularly because of the extension of patronage which a nominated and paid Upper Chamber would produce, and also of the political power which the proposal would place in the hands of the cross-bench voting members of the House. With the exception of the two front benches, which were united in support of the measure, members who spoke in the debate were overwhelmingly hostile. With the imposition of a three-line whip by the Government, and on a free vote by the Conservative and Liberal parties, the motion to reject the White Paper was defeated by 270 votes to 159.

Southern Rhodesia (United Nations Sanctions) Order 1968 was rejected by the Lords at the suggestion of the Conservative opposition leadership in that House. By that time, substantial agreement had been reached between the parties on proposals for a comprehensive reform of both the composition and the powers of the House of Lords. Despite the fact that the opposition parties were not committed to these proposals, because of the breaking-off of the conference, the Government decided to proceed with the scheme as worked out in the conference. It published in November 1968 a White Paper, 'House of Lords Reform', which faithfully reflected in all essential details the outcome of the talks.

The 1968 Government White Paper proposed a two-tier House, consisting of a first tier of some 230 voting, created peers who would have to fulfil certain requirements (principally concerning regularity of attendance), and a second tier of non-voting members who would be able to play a full part in debates and in committees but who would not be entitled to vote. Succession to a peerage was no longer to carry the right to a seat in the House, but existing peers by succession would be non-voting members of the reformed House, or might be created life

Despite the opposition shown during the debate on the White Paper in the Commons, the Government decided to honour its manifesto pledge, reiterated in the Queen's Speech opening that session. Accordingly, the Parliament (No. 2) Bill was introduced in 1968, to make the necessary legislative provision for the constitutional changes required to implement the White Paper proposals. On a Government two-line whip and a free vote by the Conservative and Liberal parties, the Bill received a Second Reading in the Commons on 3 February 1969 and was passed by 285 votes to 185, a lower majority than that for the White Paper in the previous autumn. As this was a constitutional Bill, its committee stage was taken on the floor of the House of Commons, a procedure which offered the Bill's opponents the opportunity to prolong proceedings and table a large number of amendments. The Opposition did not co-operate to impose a guillotine; and after the House had spent eleven days in committee (over 80 hours) and only the preamble and the first five clauses (out of 20) had been considered, the Prime Minister announced the abandonment of the Bill on 17 April 1969.

iii. LIST OF MEMBERS OF THE HOUSE OF LORDS
(at 1st April 1998)

Key to titles

Abp	Archbishop	**E**	Earl
B	Baroness	**L**	Baron/Lord
Bp	Bishop	**Ly**	Lady
C	Countess	**M**	Marquess
D	Duke	**V**	Viscount

Notes and abbreviations

The first column to the right of the title states the lord's party affiliation. Party allegiance is shown only when the lord is in receipt of a party whip. Independent peers who have notified the Convenor of the Cross-Bench Peers are shown as cross-benchers (**XB**). Abbreviation for affiliations are as follows:

Con	Conservative	**LibDem**	Liberal Democrat
Lab	Labour	**XB**	cross-bench

The third column shows the number of days on which the lord attended the House during the 1996-7 session. This session had 79 sitting days – an asterisk against the attendance indicates that the lord took the seat or was introduced into the House either during the course of the session 1996-7 (with maximum attendance therefore restricted) or during the current session. Totals do not include attendance for judicial or formal business, select committee meetings or swearing-in days. Numbers may be lower than actual attendance since the totals are counted before the time limit for claiming attendance has expired.

The fourth column indicates the type of peerage the lord holds. Abbreviations are as follows:

H	a hereditary peer by succession – i.e. a peer who has inherited a peerage (or has successfully claimed a dormant/abeyant hereditary title).
Cr Life	a peer whose peerage has been created in their own lifetime. Such a lord has probably received a life peerage in one of the periodical honours lists.
Cr App	a created peer whose life peerage has been given under the Appellate Jurisdiction Act and enables the title holder to become a Law Lord and hear appeals to the House of Lords from the Courts.
Cr H	a hereditary peer of first creation (a peerage that has been bestowed rather than gained by succession).
Bp	a Lord Spiritual – one of the 26 Anglican bishops and archbishops who sit in the House.

The fifth and sixth columns indicate the following:

O	The lord has chosen not to take the Oath of Allegiance in this Parliament and therefore may not sit, speak or vote in the House.
A	The lord is on leave of absence. A lord on leave of absence is expected not to attend the House.

Title	Party	attendance	peerage type	oath	leave of absence
Aberconway, L	Con	0	H	O	
Abercorn, D	Con	14	H		
Aberdare, L	Con	76	H		
Aberdeen and Temair, M	XB	0	H		
Abergavenny, M	XB	0	H	O	
Abinger, L	Con	19	H		
Ackner, L	XB	69	Cr App		
Acton, L	Lab	49	H		
Addington, L	LibDem	79	H		
Addison, V	Con	76	H		
Ailesbury, M	XB	70	H		
Ailsa, M	Con	78	H		
Airlie, E	XB	2	H		
Alanbrooke, V	XB	4	H		
Albemarle, E	XB	0	H		
Aldenham, L	Con	8	H		
Alderdice, L	LibDem	31*	Cr Life		
Aldington, L	Con	42	Cr H		
Alexander of Tunis, E	Con	75	H		
Alexander of Weedon, L	Con	7	Cr Life		
Allen of Abbeydale, L	XB	44	Cr Life		
Allenby of Megiddo, V	XB	69	H		
Allendale, V	Con	0	H	O	
Alport, L		18	Cr Life		
Alton of Liverpool, L	XB	0*	Cr Life		
Alvingham, L		0	H	O	
Amherst of Hackney, L	XB	2	H		
Amos, B	Lab	0*	Cr Life		
Ampthill, L	XB	73	H		
Amwell, L	XB	3	H		
Anelay of St. Johns, B	Con	66*	Cr Life		
Anglesey, M	XB	0	H	O	
Annaly, L	Con	55	H		
Annan, L	XB	73	Cr Life		
Annandale and Hartfell, E	Con	0	H		
Arbuthnott, V	XB	0	H	O	
Archer of Sandwell, L	Lab	57	Cr Life		
Archer of Weston-Super-Mare, L	Con	40	Cr Life		
Argyll, D	Con	0	H		
Armstrong of Ilminster, L	XB	2	Cr Life		
Arran, E	Con	33	H		
Ashbourne, L	Con	71	H		
Ashburton, L	XB	11	H		
Ashcombe, L		0	H		
Ashley of Stoke, L	Lab	62	Cr Life		
Ashton of Hyde, L	XB	0	H	O	
Astor, V	Con	34	H		

THE LORD WILBERFORCE: A former Senior Law Lord and a Fellow of All Souls, Lord Wilberforce descends from the famous Wilberforce family, a fact that he always plays down. When a judge, he was reputed to have a sign that he always put on his desk in court which read 'Remember, you are paid to be bored'

THE LORD HAILSHAM: The former Lord Chancellor and Fellow of All Souls comes from a family famous for its paternalistic Toryism. Those who have stood next to him in divine service know him to be a lusty, if not deeply musical, singer of hymns

THE LORD PAUL: Little can his ancestors in the Punjab have imagined that their descendant would one day become not only one of the wealthiest men in Britain but sit in the House of Lords. He is a generous supporter of many youth-based projects

Title	Party	attendance	peerage type	oath	leave of absence
Astor of Hever, L	**Con**	75	H		
Atholl, D		0	H	O	
Attenborough, L	**Lab**	0	Cr Life		
Attlee, E	**Con**	77	H		
Auckland, L		0	H	O	
Avebury, L	**LibDem**	65	H		
Aylesford, E	**Con**	0	H		
Baden-Powell, L		0	H	O	A
Bagot, L		0	H		
Bagri, L	**Con**	2*	Cr Life		
Baillieu, L		0	H	O	A
Baker of Dorking, L	**Con**	0*	Cr Life		
Baldwin of Bewdley, E	**XB**	51	H		
Balfour, E	**Con**	48	H		
Balfour of Burleigh, L	**XB**	11	H		
Balfour of Inchrye, L	**XB**	2	H		
Banbury of Southam, L	**Con**	27	H		
Barber, L	**Con**	9	Cr Life		
Barber of Tewkesbury, L	**XB**	50	Cr Life		
Barnard, L	**XB**	9	H		
Barnett, L	**Lab**	63	Cr Life		
Basing, L		0	H	O	
Bassam of Brighton, L	**Lab**	0*	Cr Life		
Bath, M	**LibDem**	14	H		
Bath and Wells, Bp		0*	Bp		
Bathurst, E	**Con**	9	H		
Bauer, L	**Con**	5	Cr Life		
Bearsted, V	**Con**	7*	H		
Beatty, E		0	H	O	
Beaufort, D	**Con**	0	H	O	
Beaumont of Whitley, L	**LibDem**	77	Cr Life		
Beaverbrook, L	**Con**	48	H		
Bedford, D		0	H	O	
Belhaven and Stenton, L	**Con**	79	H		
Bellwin, L	**Con**	23	Cr Life		
Beloff, L	**Con**	71	Cr Life		
Belper, L		0	H	O	
Belstead, L	**Con**	27	H		
Berkeley, L	**Lab**	71	H		
Berners, B	**Con**	28	H		
Bessborough, E		0	H	O	A
Bethell, L	**Con**	37	H		
Bicester, L		0	H	O	
Biddulph, L	**Con**	22	H		
Biffen, L	**Con**	0*	Cr Life		
Bingham of Cornhill, L	**XB**	8	Cr Life		
Birdwood, L	**Con**	70	H		

THE BARONESS DEAN: *Former General Secretary of the printers' union SOGAT,
she is regarded as a 'fiesty lady', and respected as such. She lists 'thinking' among her
recreations, perhaps because there is so little time for it in a life as busy as hers*

THE LORD MARLESFORD: *Before his elevation
to the peerage in 1991, Mark Marlesford
was one of the anonymous contributors
to that most distinguished of papers,
The Economist. Unusually, he has
combined a career of journalism with
farming in Suffolk and rural campaigning,
as President of the Council
for the Protection of Rural England.
His aristocratic mien gives warning that
he is an unconventional Conservative*

THE LORD INGLEWOOD:
*After a spell in the European
Parliament, he became
a junior minister in the
Conservative administration,
he had a way of answering
questions that made the
questioner feel his contribution
was of genuine interest*

Title	Party	attendance	peerage type	oath	leave of absence
Birkett, L	XB	2	H		
Birmingham, Bp		3	Bp		
Blackburn, Bp		14	Bp		
Blackstone, B	Lab	71	Cr Life		
Blackwell, L	Con	0*	Cr Life		
Blake, L	Con	21	Cr Life		
Blakenham, V	Con	1	H		
Blaker, L	Con	38	Cr Life		
Blatch, B	Con	65	Cr Life		
Blease, L	Lab	48	Cr Life		
Bledisloe, V	XB	8	H		
Blyth, L	XB	59	H		
Blyth of Rowington, L	Con	1	Cr Life		
Boardma.., L	Con	39	Cr Life		
Bolingbroke and St John, V		0	H	O	
Bolton, L	Con	1	H		
Borrie, L	Lab	73	Cr Life		
Borthwick, L	XB	0*	H		
Borwick, L		0	H	O	A
Boston, L	Con	0	H	O	
Boston of Faversham, L	XB	78	Cr Life		
Bowness, L	Con	60	Cr Life		
Boyd of Merton, V		0	H	O	A
Boyd-Carpenter, L	Con	41	Cr Life		
Boyne, V	XB	0	H	O	
Brabazon of Tara, L	Con	72	H		
Brabourne, L	XB	0	H	O	
Bradbury, L	Con	0	H		
Bradford, E	Con	17	H		
Bradford, Bp		0*	Bp		
Brain, L	XB	24	H		
Braine of Wheatley, L	Con	31	Cr Life		
Bramall, L	XB	19	Cr Life		
Brandon of Oakbrook, L	XB	0	Cr App	O	
Brassey of Apethorpe, L	Con	0	H	O	
Braybrooke, L	Con	8	H		
Braye, B		0	H		
Brentford, V	Con	66	H		
Bridge of Harwich, L	XB	5	Cr App		
Bridgeman, V	Con	48	H		
Bridges, L	XB	42	H		
Bridport, V		0	H	O	A
Briggs, L	XB	4	Cr Life		
Brightman, L	XB	65	Cr App		
Brigstocke, B	Con	48	Cr Life		
Bristol, M		0	H	O	
Bristol, Bp		6	Bp		
Broadbridge, L	XB	75	H		
Brocket, L		0	H	O	

TOP LEFT: THE LORD JAKOBOVITS: *The proud progenitor of 40 grandchildren, the former Chief Rabbi holds old-fashioned views on the family. He is one of the few practising Jews to have been made a peer*

TOP RIGHT: THE BARONESS TRUMPINGTON: *A Bletchley girl during the Second World War, Lady Trumpington came to the Lords from local government. Despite her formidable appearance and self-confessedly bossy manner, she is regarded with great affection throughout the House. When a Government spokesman she made up for any lack of briefing with her wit*

LEFT: THE LORD JENKINS OF HILLHEAD: *After a dazzling career in the Commons, in the course of which he was Home Secretary and Chancellor of the Exchequer in the Labour Government, Lord Jenkins became a founding member of the Liberal Democrats and has been leader of that party in the Lords. He combines politics and literature along with an enjoyment of good living*

Title	Party	attendance	peerage type	oath	leave of absence
Brooke and Warwick, E		1*	H	O	A
Brooke of Alverthorpe, L	Lab	0*	Cr Life		
Brooke of Ystradfellte, B		0	Cr Life	O	A
Brookeborough, V	XB	24	H		
Brookes, L	XB	21	Cr Life		
Brooks of Tremorfa, L	Lab	74	Cr Life		
Brougham and Vaux, L	Con	79	H		
Broughshane, L	XB	30	H		
Browne-Wilkinson, L	XB	15	Cr App		
Brownlow, L		0	H	O	A
Bruce of Donington, L	Lab	79	Cr Life		
Bruntisfield, L	Con	55	H		
Buccleuch and Queensberry, D	Con	3	H		
Buchan, E	XB	8	H		
Buckinghamshire, E	Con	19	H		
Buckmaster, V	XB	0	H	O	
Bullock, L	XB	0	Cr Life	O	
Burden, L		0	H	O	
Burgh, L		0	H	O	
Burlison, L	Lab	0*	Cr Life		
Burnham, L	Con	68	H		
Burton, L	Con	9	H		
Bute, M		0	H	O	
Butler of Brockwell, L		0*	Cr Life		
Butterfield, L	Con	39	Cr Life		
Butterworth, L	Con	73	Cr Life		
Buxton of Alsa, L	Con	3	Cr Life		
Byford, B	Con	55*	Cr Life		
Byron, L	Con	3	H		
Cadman, L	Con	78	H		
Cadogan, E	Con	0*	H		
Cairns, E	XB	0	H		
Caithness, E	Con	60	H		
Caldecote, V	Con	22	H		
Callaghan of Cardiff, L	Lab	58	Cr Life		
Calverley, L	LibDem	36*	H		
Camden, M		0	H	O	A
Cameron of Lochbroom, L	XB	5	Cr Life		
Camoys, L	XB	3	H		
Campbell of Alloway, L	Con	79	Cr Life		
Campbell of Croy, L	Con	78	Cr Life		
Canterbury, Abp		4	Bp		
Carew, L	XB	21	H		
Carlisle, E	LibDem	42	H		
Carlisle, Bp		16	Bp		
Carlisle of Bucklow, L	Con	28	Cr Life		
Carmichael of Kelvingrove, L	Lab	73	Cr Life		

Title	Party	attendance	peerage type	oath	leave of absence
Carnarvon, E	XB	25	H		
Carnegy of Lour, B	Con	62	Cr Life		
Carnock, L	Con	57	H		
Carr of Hadley, L	Con	40	Cr Life		
Carrick, E	XB	0*	H		
Carrington, L	Con	5	H		
Carter, L	Lab	65	Cr Life		
Carver, L	XB	25	Cr Life		
Castle of Blackburn, B	Lab	20	Cr Life		
Cathcart, E	Con	0	H	O	
Catto, L		0	H	O	
Cavendish of Furness, L	Con	11	Cr Life		
Cawdor, E	XB	1*	H	O	
Cawley, L	Con	0	H		
Cayzer, L		0	Cr Life	O	A
Chadlington, L	Con	39*	Cr Life		
Chalfont, L	XB	61	Cr Life		
Chalker of Wallasey, B	Con	39	Cr Life		
Chandos, V	Lab	14	H		
Chapple, L	XB	33	Cr Life		
Charteris of Amisfield, L	XB	69	Cr Life		
Chatfield, L		0	H	O	A
Chelmsford, V	Con	36	H		
Chesham, L	Con	76	H		
Chetwode, L		0	H		
Chichester, E	Con	0	H	O	
Chichester, Bp		25	Bp		
Chilston, V	Con	0	H		
Chilver, L	Con	0	Cr Life		
Chitnis, L	XB	0	Cr Life	O	
Cholmondeley, M	XB	0	H	O	
Chorley, L	XB	54	H		
Churchill, V		0	H	O	
Churston, L	Con	0	H		
Citrine, L		0	H	O	
Clancarty, E	XB	63	H		
Clanwilliam, E	Con	67	H		
Clarendon, E		0	H		
Clark of Kempston, L	Con	68	Cr Life		
Cledwyn of Penrhos, L	Lab	75	Cr Life		
Clifford of Chudleigh, L	XB	10	H		
Clinton, L	Con	9	H		
Clinton-Davis, L	Lab	65	Cr Life		
Clitheroe, L		9	H	O	A
Clwyd, L	XB	5	H		
Clyde, L	XB	27	Cr App		
Clydesmuir, L		0	H	O	
Cobbold, L	XB	20	H		

Title	Party	attendance	peerage type	oath	leave of absence
Cobham, V		0	H	O	A
Cochrane of Cults, L	Con	27	H		
Cockfield, L	Con	68	Cr Life		
Cocks of Hartcliffe, L	Lab	78	Cr Life		
Coggan, L	XB	0	Cr Life		
Coleraine, L	Con	64	H		
Coleridge, L	Con	42	H		
Colgrain, L	XB	0	H		
Colville of Culross, V	XB	46	H		
Colwyn, L	Con	67	H		
Colyton, L		0	H	O	
Combermere, V	XB	0	H	O	
Congleton, L	XB	18	H		
Constantine of Stanmore, L	Con	65	Cr Life		
Conyngham, M		0	H	O	
Cooke of Islandreagh, L	XB	17	Cr Life		
Cooke of Thorndon, L	XB	15	Cr Life		
Cope of Berkeley, L	Con	0*	Cr Life		
Cork and Orrery, E	Con	5	H		
Cornwallis, L	XB	22	H		
Cottenham, E	Con	0	H	O	
Cottesloe, L	XB	11	H		
Courtown, E	Con	76	H		
Coventry, E	Con	2	H	O	
Cowdray, V	XB	0*	H		
Cowdrey of Tonbridge, L	Con	0*	Cr Life		
Cowley, E	Con	20	H		
Cox, B	Con	46	Cr Life		
Craig of Radley, L	XB	63	Cr Life		
Craigavon, V	XB	69	H		
Craigmyle, L	Con	10	H		
Cranborne, V	Con	73	H		
Cranbrook, E	Con	21	H		
Cranworth, L	Con	5	H		
Crathorne, L	Con	54	H		
Craven, E		0	H	O	
Crawford and Balcarres, E	Con	1	H		
Crawshaw, L		0	H	O	
Crickhowell, L	Con	59	Cr Life		
Croft, L		0	H	O	
Croham, L	XB	14	Cr Life		
Cromartie, E	XB	4	H		
Cromer, E	Con	31	H	O	
Cromwell, L	XB	0	H		
Crook, L	XB	12	H		
Cross, V	Con	71	H		
Cuckney, L	Con	55	Cr Life		
Cudlipp, L	LibDem	0	Cr Life		

THE LORD BOSTON OF FAVERSHAM: *A former Labour M.P. the Chairman of Commitees is a man of immense courtesy. His mild exterior does not suggest the strength that lies within*

THE LORD IVEAGH: *Scion of the Guinness brewing family, Lord Iveagh is one of the youngest members of the House. His maiden speech campaigned for improvements to the legal status of the citizens of the island of St Helena; however, they were refused passports by the House of Commons*

Title	Party	attendance	peerage type	oath	leave of absence
Cullen of Ashbourne, L	Con	67	H		
Cumberlege, B	Con	56	Cr Life		
Cunliffe, L	XB	0	H		
Currie of Marylebone, L	Lab	43*	Cr Life		
Dacre, B	XB	2	H		
Dacre of Glanton, L	Con	21	Cr Life		
Dahrendorf, L	LibDem	31	Cr Life		
Dalhousie, E		0	H	O	
Darcy de Knayth, B	XB	48	H		
Daresbury, L		1*	H		
Darling, L		0	H	O	A
Darnley, E	Con	0	H		
Dartmouth, E		0	H		
Darwen, L		0	H	O	
Daventry, V	Con	2	H		
David, B	Lab	73	Cr Life		
Davidson, V	Con	79	H		
Davies, L	LibDem	4	H		
Davies of Coity, L	Lab	0*	Cr Life		
Davies of Oldham, L	Lab	0*	Cr Life		
de Clifford, L		0	H	O	
De Freyne, L	Con	57	H		
De La Warr, E	Con	0	H		
De L'Isle, V	Con	1	H		
De Mauley, L		0	H	O	A
De Ramsey, L	Con	3	H		
De Ros, L		0	H	O	
De Saumarez, L	Con	4	H		
de Villiers, L		0	H	O	
Dean of Beswick, L	Lab	79	Cr Life		
Dean of Harptree, L	Con	73	Cr Life		
Dean of Thornton-le-Fylde, B	Lab	51	Cr Life		
Dearing, L		0*	Cr Life		
Deedes, L	Con	1	Cr Life		
Delacourt-Smith of Alteryn, B	Lab	0	Cr Life	O	
Delamere, L		0	H	O	
Denbigh, E	Con	51*	H		
Denham, L	Con	63	H		
Denington, B	Lab	0	Cr Life	O	
Denman, L	Con	4	H		
Denning, L	XB	0	Cr App	O	
Denton of Wakefield, B	Con	31	Cr Life		
Deramore, L		0	H	O	A
Derby, E	XB	0	H		
Derwent, L	Con	17	H		
Desai, L	Lab	63	Cr Life		
Devon, E		0	H	O	

Title	Party	attendance	peerage type	oath	leave of absence
Devonport, V	XB	26	H		
Devonshire, D	XB	3	H		
Dholakia, L	LibDem	0*	Cr Life		
Diamond, L	Lab	11	Cr Life		
Dickinson, L	XB	1	H		
Digby, L	Con	5	H		
Dilhorne, V	Con	58	H		
Dinevor, L		0	H	O	
Dixon, L	Lab	0*	Cr Life		
Dixon-Smith, L	Con	77	Cr Life		
Donaldson of Lymington, L	XB	19	Cr Life		
Donegall, M	Con	18	H		
Donoughmore, E	Con	1	H		
Donoughue, L	Lab	68	Cr Life		
Dormand of Easington, L	Lab	78	Cr Life		
Dormer, L		0	H	O	
Dowding, L	XB	8	H		
Downe, V		0	H	O	
Downshire, M	Con	39	H		
Drogheda, E	XB	17	H		
Dubs, L	Lab	78	Cr Life		
Ducie, E		0	H	O	
Dudley, E	Con	12	H		
Dudley, B		0	H	O	A
Dulverton, L	XB	2	H		
Dundee, E	Con	49	H		
Dundonald, E	Con	26	H		
Dunleath, L	XB	0	H		
Dunmore, E		0	H	O	
Dunn, B	XB	2	Cr Life		
Dunrossil, V	XB	19	H		
Durham, Bp		11	Bp		
Dysart, C		0	H	O	
Eames, L	XB	9	Cr Life		
Eatwell, L	Lab	45	Cr Life		
Ebury, L		0	H	O	
Eccles, V	Con	5	Cr H		
Eccles of Moulton, B	Con	30	Cr Life		
Eden of Winton, L	Con	28	Cr Life		
Edinburgh, D	XB	0	Cr H	O	
Effingham, E	XB	19	H		
Eglinton, E		0	H		
Egmont, E		0	H	O	
Eldon, E	XB	0	H	O	
Elgin and Kincardine, E	Con	0	H		
Elibank, L	Con	25	H		
Elis-Thomas, L	XB	54	Cr Life		

Title	Party	attendance	peerage type	oath	leave of absence
Ellenborough, L	Con	66	H		
Elles, B	Con	68	Cr Life		
Elliott of Morpeth, L	Con	76	Cr Life		
Elphinstone, L		0	H	O	
Elton, L	Con	72	H		
Ely, M		0	H		
Ely, Bp		5*	Bp		
Elystan-Morgan, L		0	Cr Life	O	A
Emerton, B	XB	4*	Cr Life		
Emslie, L	XB	0	Cr Life		
Enniskillen, E	XB	10	H		
Erne, E	Con	40	H		
Erroll, E	XB	57	H		
Erroll of Hale, L	Con	16	Cr H		
Esher, V		0	H	O	A
Essex, E	XB	0	H	O	
Evans of Parkside, L	Lab	0*	Cr Life		
Ewing of Kirkford, L	Lab	19	Cr Life		
Exeter, M	XB	0	H		
Exeter, Bp		9	Bp		
Exmouth, V	XB	54	H		
Ezra, L	LibDem	74	Cr Life		
Fairfax of Cameron, L	Con	19	H		
Fairhaven, L	Con	2	H		
Falconer of Thoroton, L	Lab	0*	Cr Life		
Falkender, B	Lab	13	Cr Life		
Falkland, V	LibDem	71	H		
Falmouth, V	Con	1	H		
Fanshawe of Richmond, L	Con	6	Cr Life		
Faringdon, L	XB	0	H		
Farrington of Ribbleton, B	Lab	66	Cr Life		
Feldman, L	Con	39	Cr Life		
Ferrers, E	Con	65	H		
Feversham, L	XB	9	H		
Fife, D		1	H		
Fisher, L		0	H		
Fisher of Rednal, B	Lab	31	Cr Life		
Fitt, L		78	Cr Life		
FitzWalter, L		0	H		
Flather, B	Con	68	Cr Life		
Flowers, L	XB	10	Cr Life		
Foley, L		0	H		
Fookes, B	Con	0*	Cr Life		
Foot, L	LibDem	0	Cr Life	O	
Forbes, L	Con	14	H		
Forester, L	Con	0	H		
Forres, L	XB	0	H	O	

LEFT: THE LORD BELOFF: A thorough-going academic and former Fellow of All Souls, Lord Beloff displays the academic's total disregard for his appearance. A Conservative, he enunciates his views without notes and with complete disregard for his party's official policy

BELOW: THE LORD WEATHERILL: Lord Weatherill's father, a tailor, led the last successful strike of Savile Row tailors against sweatshop conditions in 1912. He was for abolishing the House of Lords. Lord Weatherill, however, describes himself as a convert to it, as well as to the hereditary system. He was Speaker in the House of Commons, 1983-92

THE BARONESS HYLTON-FOSTER: Lady Hylton-Foster, the previous Convener of the Cross-Bench Peers, had a father and a husband who were both Speakers of the House of Commons

Title	Party	attendance	peerage type	oath	leave of absence
Forte, L	Con	0	Cr Life		
Fortescue, E	Con	3	H		
Forteviot, L	Con	1	H		
Fraser of Carmyllie, L	Con	36	Cr Life		
Freeman, L	Con	0*	Cr Life		
Freyberg, L	XB	65	H		
Gage, V	Con	16	H		
Gainford, L	Con	76	H		
Gainsborough, E	XB	36	H		
Gallacher, L	Lab	66	Cr Life		
Galloway, E	Con	0	H	O	
Gardner of Parkes, B	Con	62	Cr Life		
Garel-Jones, L	Con	0*	Cr Life		
Geddes, L	Con	55	H		
Geraint, L	LibDem	76	Cr Life		
Gerard, L	XB	9	H		
Gibson, L	XB	12	Cr Life		
Gibson-Watt, L	Con	12	Cr Life		
Gifford, L	Lab	4	H		
Gilbert, L	Lab	0*	Cr Life		
Gillmore of Thamesfield, L	XB	38	Cr Life		
Gilmour of Craigmillar, L	Con	21	Cr Life		
Gisborough, L	Con	49	H		
Gladwin of Clee, L	Lab	75	Cr Life		
Gladwyn, L	XB	28*	H		
Glanusk, L		0	H		
Glasgow, E	LibDem	9	H		
Glenamara, L	Lab	35	Cr Life		
Glenarthur, L	Con	41	H		
Glenconner, L	LibDem	0	H	O	
Glendevon, L		0	H	O	
Glendyne, L	Con	1	H		
Glentoran, L	Con	25	H		
Gloucester, D	XB	0	H		
Gloucester, Bp		0*	Bp	O	
Goff of Chieveley, L	XB	8	Cr App		
Goodhart, L	LibDem	0*	Cr Life		
Gordon of Strathblane, L	Lab	0*	Cr Life		
Gorell, L	XB	1	H		
Gormanston, V	Con	1	H		
Goschen, V	Con	56	H		
Gosford, E	XB	0	H	O	
Gough, V	XB	0	H	O	
Gould of Potternewton, B	Lab	73	Cr Life		
Gowrie, E	Con	34	H		
Grade, L	XB	0	Cr Life		
Grafton, D	Con	0	H		

Title	Party	Attendance	Peerage Type	Oath	Leave of Absence
Graham of Edmonton, L	Lab	78	Cr Life		
Granard, E	Con	7	H		
Grantchester, L	Lab	22	H		
Grantley, L	XB	3	H		
Granville, E		0	H	O	
Gray, L	Con	24	H		
Gray of Contin, L	Con	56	Cr Life		
Greene of Harrow Weald, L	Lab	6	Cr Life		
Greenhill, L		0	H	O	
Greenhill of Harrow, L	XB	47	Cr Life		
Greenway, L	XB	74	H		
Greenwood, V		0	H	O	A
Gregson, L	Lab	42	Cr Life		
Grenfell, L	Lab	37	H		
Gretton, L		0	H	O	
Grey, E	LibDem	74	H		
Grey of Codnor, L		0	H	O	
Grey of Naunton, L	XB	0	Cr Life	O	
Gridley, L	LibDem	0*	H		
Griffiths, L	XB	6	Cr App		
Griffiths of Fforestfach, L	Con	13	Cr Life		
Grimston of Westbury, L	Con	18	H		
Grimthorpe, L	Con	2	H	O	
Guilford, E		0	H		
Habgood, L	XB	12	Cr Life		
Hacking, L	Con	48	H		
Haddington, E	Con	21	H		
Haden-Guest, L		0*	H		
Haig, E	Con	14	H		
Hailsham of Saint Marylebone, L	Con	66	Cr Life		
Halifax, E	Con	3	H		
Halsbury, E	XB	71	H		
Hambleden, V	Con	0	H	O	
Hambro, L	Con	1	Cr Life		
Hamilton and Brandon, D	XB	0	H	O	
Hamilton of Dalzell, L	Con	10	H		
Hamlyn, L		0*	Cr Life		
Hampden, V	XB	7	H		
Hampton, L	LibDem	18	H		
Hamwee, B	LibDem	42	Cr Life		
Hankey, L	XB	17*	H		
Hanson, L	Con	5	Cr Life		
Hanworth, V	Lab	26*	H		
Hardie, L	Lab	0*	Cr Life		
Harding of Petherton, L	Con	77	H		
Hardinge, V	XB	0	H	O	
Hardinge of Penshurst, L		0*	H		

Title	Party	attendance	peerage type	oath	leave of absence
Hardwicke, E	Con	48	H		
Hardy of Wath, L	Lab	0*	Cr Life		
Harewood, E		0	H	O	
Harlech, L	Con	39	H		
Harmar-Nicholls, L	Con	54	Cr Life		
Harmsworth, L	Con	27	H		
Harrington, E		0	H	O	A
Harris, L		0	H	O	
Harris of Greenwich, L	LibDem	79	Cr Life		
Harris of High Cross, L	XB	23	Cr Life		
Harris of Peckham, L	Con	18	Cr Life		
Harrowby, E	Con	38	H		
Hartwell, L	XB	0	Cr Life		
Harvey of Tasburgh, L	Con	0	H	O	
Haskel, L	Lab	74	Cr Life		
Haslam, L	Con	24	Cr Life		
Hastings, L	Con	5	H		
Hatherton, L		0	H	O	
Hattersley, L	Lab	0*	Cr Life		
Hawke, L	Con	3*	H		
Hayhoe, L	Con	78	Cr Life		
Hayman, B	Lab	68	Cr Life		
Hayter, L	XB	69	H		
Hazlerigg, L		0	H	O	A
Head, V	XB	0	H		
Headfort, M	XB	1	H		
Healey, L	Lab	45	Cr Life		
Hemingford, L	XB	1	H		
Hemphill, L	Con	31	H		
Henderson of Brompton, L	XB	38	Cr Life		
Henley, L	Con	51	H		
Henniker, L	XB	4	H		
Hereford, V		0	H	O	
Hereford, Bp		9*	Bp		
Herries, Ly		0	H	O	
Herschell, L		0	H	O	A
Hertford, M		0*	H	O	
Hesketh, L	Con	9	H		
Heytesbury, L		0	H	O	
Higgins, L	Con	0*	Cr Life		
Hill, V		0	H	O	A
Hill-Norton, L	XB	3	Cr Life		
Hilton of Eggardon, B	Lab	74	Cr Life		
Hindlip, L	Con	12	H		
Hives, L	XB	0	H		
Hoffmann, L	XB	17	Cr App		
Hogg, B	Con	16	Cr Life		
Hogg of Cumbernauld, L	Lab	0*	Cr Life		

BELOW: THE BARONESS HOLLIS OF HEIGHAM: University lecturer and a Labour activist in local government, author of several books, including The Pauper Press; Class & Conflict, 1815-1850; Women in Public; Ladies Elect *and* Women in English Local Government 1865-1914

ABOVE: THE BARONESS DUNN: Elegant in her looks and in her dress, Baroness Dunn is the epitome of the Hong Kong Chinese. A QC, greatly respected in Hong Kong where she served on the Executive Council for many years and a director of many European companies, she can truly be said to bestride two cultures

Title	Party	attendance	peerage type	oath	leave of absence
Holderness, L	Con	78	Cr Life		
Hollenden, L		0	H	O	A
Hollick, L	Lab	12	Cr Life		
Hollis of Heigham, B	Lab	75	Cr Life		
Holme of Cheltenham, L	LibDem	54	Cr Life		
HolmPatrick, L	Con	77	H		
Home, E	Con	16*	H		
Hood, V	Con	20	H		
Hooper, B	Con	57	Cr Life		
Hooson, L	LibDem	70	Cr Life		
Hope of Craighead, L	XB	45	Cr Life		
Hothfield, L	Con	18	H		
Howard de Walden, L		0	H	O	A
Howard of Penrith, L		0	H	O	A
Howe, E	Con	44	H		
Howe of Aberavon, L	Con	8	Cr Life		
Howell, L	Lab	37	Cr Life		
Howell of Guildford, L	Con	0*	Cr Life		
Howick of Glendale, L		0	H	O	
Howie of Troon, L	Lab	61	Cr Life		
Hoyle, L	Lab	0*	Cr Life		
Hughes, L	Lab	69	Cr Life		
Hughes of Woodside, L	Lab	0*	Cr Life		
Hunt, L	LibDem	10	Cr Life		
Hunt of Kings Heath, L	Lab	0*	Cr Life		
Hunt of Tanworth, L	XB	24	Cr Life		
Hunt of Wirral, L	Con	0*	Cr Life		
Huntingdon, E	XB	8	H		
Huntly, M	Con	10	H		
Hurd of Westwell, L	Con	0*	Cr Life		
Hussey of North Bradley, L	XB	43*	Cr Life		
Hutchinson of Lullington, L	LibDem	24	Cr Life		
Hutton, L	XB	5*	Cr App		
Hylton, L	XB	52	H		
Hylton-Foster, B	XB	72	Cr Life		
Iddesleigh, E	XB	5	H		
Ilchester, E	XB	63	H		
Iliffe, L		0	H		
Inchcape, E	Con	39	H		
Inchyra, L	XB	38	H		
Inge, L	XB	0*	Cr Life		
Ingleby, V	XB	15	H		
Inglewood, L	Con	55	H		
Ingrow, L	Con	1	Cr Life	O	
Inverforth, L		0	H	O	
Ironside, L	Con	63	H		
Irvine of Lairg, L	Lab	35	Cr Life		

Title	Party	attendance	peerage type	oath	leave of absence
Islwyn L	Lab	0*	Cr Life		
Iveagh, E	XB	1	H		
Jacobs, L	LibDem	0*	Cr Life		
Jakobovits, L	XB	9	Cr Life		
James of Holland Park, B	Con	7	Cr Life		
Janner of Braunstone, L	Lab	0*	Cr Life		
Jauncey of Tullichettle, L	XB	12	Cr App		
Jay of Paddington, B	Lab	66	Cr Life		
Jeffreys, L	Con	46	H		
Jeger, B	Lab	50	Cr Life		
Jellicoe, E	Con	54	H		
Jenkin of Roding, L	Con	59	Cr Life		
Jenkins of Hillhead, L	LibDem	52	Cr Life		
Jenkins of Putney, L	Lab	77	Cr Life		
Jersey, E		0	H	O	A
Johnston of Rockport, L	Con	56	Cr Life		
Joicey, L	XB	0	H	O	
Jopling, L	Con	0*	Cr Life		
Judd, L	Lab	62	Cr Life		
Keith of Castleacre, L	Con	0	Cr Life		
Keith of Kinkel, L	XB	9	Cr App		
Kelvedon, L	Con	0*	Cr Life		
Kemsley, V	Con	0	H	O	
Kenilworth, L	Con	56	H		
Kennedy of The Shaws, B	Lab	0*	Cr Life		
Kennet, L	Lab	63	H		
Kensington, L		0	H	O	A
Kenswood, L		0	H	O	
Kent, D	XB	0	H		
Kenyon, L	Con	6	H		
Kershaw, L		0	H		
Keyes, L	Con	18	H		
Kilbracken, L	Lab	76	H		
Killanin, L	XB	0	H	O	
Killearn, L	Con	1*	H		
Kilmarnock, L	XB	72	H		
Kilpatrick of Kincraig, L	XB	36	Cr Life		
Kimball, L	Con	59	Cr Life		
Kimberley, E	Con	2	H		
Kindersley, L	XB	2	H		
King of Wartnaby, L	Con	11	Cr Life		
Kingsdown, L	XB	7	Cr Life		
Kingsland, L	Con	57	Cr Life		
Kinloss, Ly	XB	77	H		
Kinnoull, E	Con	73	H		
Kinross, L		0	H	O	

Title	Party	attendance	peerage type	oath	leave of absence
Kintore, E	XB	43	H		
Kirkhill, L	Lab	44	Cr Life		
Kirkwood, L	LibDem	10	H		
Kitchener, E	Con	33	H		
Knight of Collingtree, B	Con	0*	Cr Life		
Knights, L	XB	8	Cr Life		
Knollys, V	Con	36	H		
Knutsford, V	Con	13	H		
Laing of Dunphail, L	Con	27	Cr Life		
Lambert, V		0	H	O	
Lane, L	XB	12	Cr App		
Lane of Horsell, L	Con	16	Cr Life		
Lang of Monkton, L	Con	0*	Cr Life		
Lansdowne, M		0	H	O	
Latham, L		0	H	O	A
Latymer, L		0	H	O	
Lauderdale, E	Con	76	H		
Lawrence, L	XB	76	H		
Lawson of Blaby, L	Con	27	Cr Life		
Layton, L	Con	59	H		
Leathers, V	XB	40	H		
Leconfield and Egremont, L	Con	0	H		
Leicester, E	XB	2*	H		
Leicester, Bp		5*	Bp		
Leigh, L	Con	55	H		
Leighton of Saint Mellons, L		0	H	O	
Leinster, D		0	H	O	A
Lester of Herne Hill, L	LibDem	37	Cr Life		
Leven and Melville, E		0	H	O	
Levene of Portsoken, L	XB	0*	Cr Life		
Leverhulme, V	Con	1	H		
Levy, L	Lab	0*	Cr Life		
Lewin, L	XB	1	Cr Life		
Lewis of Newnham, L	XB	10	Cr Life		
Lichfield, E	Con	0	H		
Lichfield, Bp		11	Bp		
Lilford, L		0	H	O	A
Limerick, E	Con	5	H		
Lincoln, E		0	H	O	
Lincoln, Bp		15	Bp		
Lindsay, E	Con	30	H		
Lindsay of Birker, L	XB	0	H	O	
Lindsey and Abingdon, E	Con	29	H		
Linklater of Butterstone, B	LibDem	0*	Cr Life		
Linlithgow, M		0	H		
Listowel, E		0	H	O	
Liverpool, E	Con	68	H		

THE EARL OF HALSBURY: *Grandson of the famous Lord Chancellor, the first earl, who died in 1921 at the age of 98; the present Lord Halsbury recently celebrated his 90th birthday*

THE BARONESS THATCHER: *As much an icon as Elizabeth I. In the Lords, she made a memorable maiden speech, which disregarded every convention; it was not only controversial but lasted 25 minutes instead of the 10 minutes customary for maiden speeches*

THE LORD CAMPBELL OF CROY: *A former Conservative MP, Secretary of State for Scotland, 1970-74, he was severely wounded in the Second World War, during which he won an MC and Bar*

Title	Party	attendance	peerage type	oath	leave of absence
Lloyd of Berwick, L	XB	18	Cr App		
Lloyd of Highbury, B	XB	0*	Cr Life		
Lloyd-George of Dwyfor, E	XB	24	H		
Lloyd-Webber, L	Con	1*	Cr Life		
Lockwood, B	Lab	59	Cr Life		
Lofthouse of Pontefract, L	Lab	0*	Cr Life		
Londesborough, L		0	H	O	
London, Bp		2	Bp		
Londonderry, M		0	H	O	
Long, V	Con	71	H		
Longford, E	Lab	78	Cr H		
Lonsdale, E	Con	0	H		
Lothian, M	Con	6	H		
Loudoun, C	XB	0	H		
Lovat, L		0	H	O	
Lovelace, E	XB	1	H	O	
Lovell-Davis, L	Lab	35	Cr Life		
Lowry, L	XB	62	Cr Life		
Lucan, E		0	H	O	
Lucas, L	Con	71	H		
Lucas of Chilworth, L	Con	70	H		
Ludford, B	LibDem	0*	Cr Life		
Luke, L	Con	57	H		
Lyell, L	Con	70	H		
Lytton, E	XB	25	H		
Lyveden, L		0	H	O	
McAlpine of West Green, L		11	Cr Life		
MacAndrew, L	Con	0	H		
Macaulay of Bragar, L	Lab	32	Cr Life	O	
McCarthy, L	Lab	28	Cr Life		
Macclesfield, E	XB	10	H		
McCluskey, L	XB	5	Cr Life		
McColl of Dulwich, L	Con	75	Cr Life		
McConnell, L	XB	61	Cr Life		
Macdonald of Gwaenysgor, L		0	H	O	
Macfarlane of Bearsden, L	Con	11	Cr Life		
McFarlane of Llandaff, B	XB	23	Cr Life		
McGowan, L		0	H		
McIntosh of Haringey, L	Lab	78	Cr Life		
Mackay of Ardbrecknish, L	Con	70	Cr Life		
Mackay of Clashfern, L	Con	78	Cr Life		
Mackay of Drumadoon, L	Con	48	Cr Life		
Mackenzie-Stuart, L	XB	0	Cr Life		
Mackie of Benshie, L	LibDem	47	Cr Life		
Mackintosh of Halifax, V	Con	9	H		
MacLaurin of Knebworth, L	Con	3*	Cr Life		
Maclay, L		0	H	O	A

Title	Party	attendance	peerage type	oath	leave of absence
MacLehose of Beoch, L	XB	19	Cr Life		
Macleod of Borve, B	Con	55	Cr Life		
McNair, L	LibDem	75	H		
McNally, L	LibDem	68	Cr Life		
Macpherson of Drumochter, L	Con	6	H		
Maddock, B	LibDem	0*	Cr Life		
Mallalieu, B	Lab	34	Cr Life		
Malmesbury, E	Con	18	H		
Malvern, V		0	H	O	
Manchester, D	XB	0	H	O	
Manchester, Bp		0	Bp		
Mancroft, L	Con	13	H		
Manners, L	Con	0	H	O	
Mansfield, E	Con	0	H		
Manton, L	Con	7	H		
Mar, C	XB	55	H		
Mar and Kellie, E	LibDem	63	H		
Marchamley, L		0	H	O	
Marchwood, V	Con	0	H		
Margadale, L		0	H	O	
Margesson, V		0	H	O	A
Marks of Broughton, L	XB	0	H	O	
Marlborough, D	Con	5	H		
Marlesford, L	Con	74	Cr Life		
Marsh, L	XB	70	Cr Life		
Martonmere, L	XB	0	H	O	
Masham of Ilton, B	XB	64	Cr Life		
Mason of Barnsley, L	Lab	70	Cr Life		
Massereene and Ferrard, V	Con	65	H		
May, L	Con	0	H		
Mayhew of Twysden, L	Con	0*	Cr Life		
Meath, E		0	H	O	A
Melchett, L		0	H	O	A
Mellish, L		0	Cr Life	O	
Melville, V	Con	8	H		
Menuhin, L	XB	0	Cr Life		
Merlyn-Rees, L	Lab	77	Cr Life		
Merrivale, L	Con	65	H		
Mersey, V	Con	73	H		
Meston, L	LibDem	50	H		
Methuen, L	LibDem	29	H		
Middleton, L	Con	22	H		
Midleton, V	XB	0	H		
Milford, L		0	H	O	A
Milford Haven, M	Con	0	H	O	
Miller of Hendon, B	Con	78	Cr Life		
Mills, V	Con	5	H		
Milne, L	XB	3	H		

Title	Party	attendance	peerage type	oath	leave of absence
Milner of Leeds, L	Lab	43	H		
Milverton, L	Con	51	H		
Minto, E	XB	8	H		
Mishcon, L	Lab	21	Cr Life		
Molloy, L	Lab	79	Cr Life		
Molyneaux of Killead, L	XB	0*	Cr Life		
Monck, V		0	H	O	
Monckton of Brenchley, V	XB	24	H		
Moncreiff, L		0	H	O	A
Monk Bretton, L	Con	23	H		
Monkswell, L	Lab	79	H		
Monro of Langholm, L	Con	0*	Cr Life		
Monson, L	XB	64	H		
Montagu of Beaulieu, L	Con	43	H		
Montague of Oxford, L	Lab	0*	Cr Life		
Monteagle of Brandon, L	Con	26	H		
Montgomery of Alamein, V	Con	54	H		
Montrose, D	Con	10	H		
Moore of Lower Marsh, L	Con	1	Cr Life		
Moore of Wolvercote, L	XB	33	Cr Life		
Moran, L	XB	63	H		
Moray, E		0*	H		
Morley, E	Con	0	H	O	
Morris, L		0	H	O	
Morris of Castle Morris, L	Lab	77	Cr Life		
Morris of Kenwood, L	XB	11	H		
Morris of Manchester, L	Lab	0*	Cr Life		
Morton, E	XB	2	H		
Mostyn, L	Con	0	H	O	
Mottistone, L	Con	71	H		
Mount Edgcumbe, E	XB	0*	H		
Mountbatten of Burma, C	XB	0	H	O	
Mountevans, L	Con	78	H		
Mountgarret, V	XB	17	H		
Mowbray and Stourton, L	Con	64	H		
Moyne, L	Con	75	H		
Moynihan, L	Con	0*	H		
Moyola, L	Con	0	Cr Life	O	
Munster, E	Con	79	H		
Murray of Epping Forest, L	Lab	54	Cr Life		
Murton of Lindisfarne, L	Con	55	Cr Life		
Mustill, L	XB	10	Cr App		
Napier and Ettrick, L	XB	71	H		
Napier of Magdala, L	XB	29	H		
Naseby, L	Con	0*	Cr Life		
Nathan, L	XB	18	H		
Neill of Bladen, L	XB	0*	Cr Life		

RIGHT: PROFESSOR THE EARL RUSSELL: *An historian of great distinction, whose books on the causes of the Civil War are the definitive works on the subject, Earl Russell stems from a tradition of politics and intellect. His father was the philosopher Bertrand Russell, and his great-grandfather, who was born in the 18th century, had the honour of proposing the Reform Bill in 1832. Earl Russell could be described as a genuine Whig, though without the fortune associated with the name. With his head of an Old Testament prophet, he is one of the best speakers in the Lords, combining wit with insight. He lists 'uxoriousness' as his recreation*

BELOW: LORD RENTON: *At the age of 90, Lord Renton shows no sign of flagging in his participation in the debates of the House. With his sharp QC's mind and alert figure, he is frequently on his feet during Question Time. This sprightliness may owe something to his recreations, listed as gardening, outdoor sports and games. He has spent a real lifetime in Parliament: for 34 years, from 1945 to 1979, he sat in the Commons as a Conservative MP; since 1979 he has sat in the Lords*

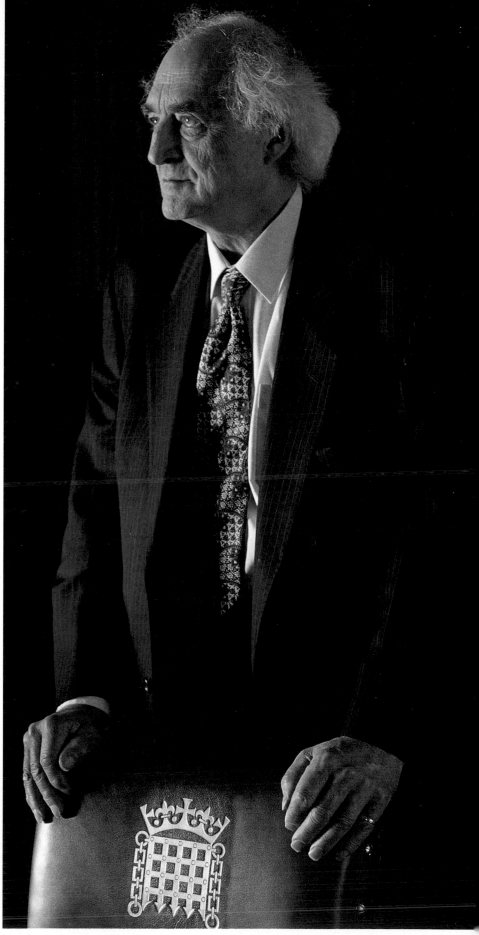

Title	Party	attendance	peerage type	oath	leave of absence
Nelson, E	XB	67	H		
Nelson of Stafford, L	XB	2	H		
Netherthorpe, L	XB	0	H		
Newall, L	Con	49	H		
Newby, L	LibDem	0*	Cr Life		
Newton, L		0	H		A
Newton of Braintree, L	Con	0*	Cr Life		
Nicholls of Birkenhead, L	XB	8	Cr App		
Nicholson of Winterbourne, B	LibDem	0*	Cr Life		
Nickson, L	Con	11	Cr Life		
Nicol, B	Lab	69	Cr Life		
Noel-Buxton, L	Con	73	H		
Nolan, L	XB	9	Cr App		
Norfolk, D	Con	26	H		
Normanby, M	XB	0	H		
Normanton, E		0	H	O	
Norrie, L	Con	69	H		
Northampton, M		0	H		
Northbourne, L	XB	48	H		
Northbrook, L	Con	7	H		
Northesk, E	Con	69	H		
Northfield, L	Lab	7	Cr Life		
Northumberland, D	XB	1	H		
Norton, L	XB	58	H		
Norwich, V		0	H	O	A
Norwich, Bp		11	Bp		
Nunburnholme, L		0	H	O	
O'Cathain, B	Con	68	Cr Life		
Ogmore, L	LibDem	44	H		
O'Hagan, L	Con	0	H	O	
Oliver of Aylmerton, L	XB	37	Cr App		
O'Neill, L		0	H		
Onslow, E	Con	36	H		
Onslow of Woking, L	Con	0*	Cr Life		
Oppenheim-Barnes, B	Con	29	Cr Life		
Oram, L	Lab	0	Cr Life	O	
Oranmore and Browne, L		0	H	O	A
Orkney, E		0*	H	O	
Orme, L	Lab	0*	Cr Life		
Orr-Ewing, L	Con	71	Cr Life		
Owen, L	XB	2	Cr Life		
Oxford, Bp		30	Bp		
Oxford and Asquith, E	XB	0	H	O	
Oxfuird, V	Con	76	H		
Palmer, L	XB	59	H		
Palumbo, L	Con	21	Cr Life		

Title	Party	attendance	peerage type	oath	leave of absence
Park of Monmouth, B	Con	73	Cr Life		
Parkinson, L	Con	14	Cr Life		
Parmoor, L		0	H	O	
Parry, L	Lab	14	Cr Life		
Patten, L	Con	0*	Cr Life		
Paul, L	Lab	59*	Cr Life		
Pearson of Rannoch, L	Con	63	Cr Life		
Peel, E	Con	41	H		
Pembroke and Montgomery, E	Con	0	H	O	
Pender, L	Con	74	H		
Penrhyn, L	Con	0	H	O	
Perry of Southwark, B	Con	40	Cr Life		
Perry of Walton, L	LibDem	59	Cr Life		
Perth, E	XB	20	H		
Peston, L	Lab	79	Cr Life		
Petre, L	XB	0	H		
Peyton of Yeovil, L	Con	52	Cr Life		
Phillimore, L	Con	1	H		
Phillips of Ellesmere, L	XB	33	Cr Life		
Piercy, L		0	H	O	
Pike, B	Con	23	Cr Life		
Pilkington of Oxenford, L	Con	71	Cr Life		
Pitkeathley, B	Lab	0*	Cr Life		
Plant of Highfield, L	Lab	51	Cr Life		
Platt of Writtle, B	Con	52	Cr Life		
Plowden, L	XB	0	Cr Life	O	
Plumb, L	Con	9	Cr Life		
Plummer of St. Marylebone, L	Con	39	Cr Life		
Plunket, L	Con	0	H		
Plymouth, E		0	H	O	A
Poltimore, L		1	H	O	A
Polwarth, L	Con	0	H		
Ponsonby of Shulbrede, L	Lab	45	H		
Poole, L	Con	5	H		
Porter of Luddenham, L	XB	39	Cr Life		
Portland, E	XB	1*	H		
Portman, V	Con	0	H		
Portsmouth, E		0	H	O	
Powerscourt, V		0	H	O	
Powis, E	XB	2	H		
Prentice, L	Con	13	Cr Life		
Prior, L	Con	27	Cr Life		
Prys-Davies, L	Lab	67	Cr Life		
Puttnam, L	Lab	0*	Cr Life		
Pym, L	Con	46	Cr Life		
Queensberry, M		0	H	O	A
Quinton, L	Con	48	Cr Life		

Title	Party	attendance	peerage type	oath	leave of absence
Quirk, L	XB	76	Cr Life		
Radnor, E	Con	0	H		
Raglan, L	XB	9	H		
Ramsay of Cartvale, B	Lab	68*	Cr Life		
Randall of St. Budeaux, L	Lab	0*	Cr Life		
Ranfurly, E	XB	2	H		
Rankeillour, L	Con	66	H		
Rathcavan, L	XB	29	H		
Rathcreedan, L	XB	15	H		
Ravensdale, L	XB	0	H	O	
Ravensworth, L		0	H	O	A
Rawlings, B	Con	47	Cr Life		
Rawlinson of Ewell, L	Con	34	Cr Life		
Rayleigh, L	Con	0	H	O	
Rayne, L	XB	1	Cr Life		
Rayner, L		0	Cr Life	O	A
Razzall, L	LibDem	0*	Cr Life		
Rea, L	Lab	77	H		
Reading, M	Con	10	H		
Reay, L	Con	48	H		
Redesdale, L	LibDem	65	H		
Rees, L	Con	59	Cr Life		
Rees-Mogg, L	XB	3	Cr Life		
Remnant, L	Con	0	H		
Rendell of Babergh, B	Lab	0*	Cr Life		
Renfrew of Kaimsthorn, L	Con	31	Cr Life		
Rennell, L	Con	66	H		
Renton, L	Con	69	Cr Life		
Renton of Mount Harry, L	Con	0*	Cr Life		
Renwick, L	Con	72	H		
Renwick of Clifton, L	Lab	0*	Cr Life		
Revelstoke, L		0	H	O	
Richard, L	Lab	68	Cr Life		
Richardson, L	XB	36	Cr Life		
Richardson of Duntisbourne, L	XB	0	Cr Life		
Richmond Lennox and Gordon, D	XB	0	H	O	
Ridley, V	XB	11	H		
Ripon, Bp		36	Bp		
Ritchie of Dundee, L	LibDem	17	H		
Riverdale, L		0	H	O	A
Rix, L	XB	47	Cr Life		
Robens of Woldingham, L		0	Cr Life	O	A
Roberts of Conwy, L	Con	0*	Cr Life		
Robertson of Oakridge, L	XB	12	H		
Roborough, L	XB	0	H	O	
Robson of Kiddington, B	LibDem	52	Cr Life		
Rochdale, V		0	H	O	

THE BARONESS STRANGE: *Baroness Strange descends from the Dukes of Athol and the Earls of Derby. The ancestor for whom the present barony was created in 1628 was later beheaded for his fidelity to the Royalist cause. Her husband, she jokes, goes one better, his being descended from a saint (St Thomas More). The idiosyncratic daughter of a greatly-respected father, who was idiosyncratic even by the standards of the Lords. She brings a weekly bouquet from her Perthshire garden for the Peers' Entrance*

THE LORD STRABOLGI: *Lord Strabolgi bears a title that was created in 1318. It fell into abeyance in 1601, until 1916 when it was claimed by Lord Strabolgi's grandfather. After Gresham's School, he was educated at the Chelsea School of Art and the Academie Scandinave, in Paris. He is knowm as a punctilious upholder of Lords traditions, but for an hereditary peer, he is unusual in taking the Labour whip. He was recently appointed as a Lord-in-waiting in the Royal Household, an office more usually occupied by government whips (these days government business leaves whips with little time for waiting). His recreations are books, music and travel*

Title	Party	attendance	peerage type	oath	leave of absence
Rochester, L	LibDem	45	H		
Rockley, L	Con	2	H		
Rodger of Earlsferry, L	XB	0	Cr Life		
Rodgers of Quarry Bank, L	LibDem	42	Cr Life		
Rodney, L	Con	18	H		
Rogers of Riverside, L	Lab	11*	Cr Life		
Roll of Ipsden, L	XB	12	Cr Life		
Rollo, L		0	H	O	
Romney, E	Con	17	H		
Rootes, L		0	H	O	
Rosebery, E		0	H	O	
Rosslyn, E	XB	16	H		
Rossmore, L		0	H	O	A
Rothermere, V		0	H		
Rotherwick, L	Con	56	H		
Rothes, E		0	H	O	A
Rothschild, L	XB	4	H		
Rowallan, L	Con	16*	H		
Roxburghe, D	Con	2	H		
Rugby, L	XB	0	H		
Runcie, L	XB	8	Cr Life		
Runciman of Doxford, V	XB	2	H		
Russell, E	LibDem	57	H		
Russell of Liverpool, L	XB	3	H		
Russell-Johnston, L	LibDem	0*	Cr Life		
Rutland, D		0	H	O	A
Ryder of Eaton Hastings, L		0	Cr Life	O	A
Ryder of Warsaw, B	XB	16	Cr Life		
Ryder of Wensum, L	Con	0*	Cr Life		
Saatchi, L	Con	20*	Cr Life		
Sackville, L	Con	0	H		
Sainsbury, L		59	Cr Life		
Sainsbury of Preston Candover, L	Con	0	Cr Life		
Sainsbury of Turville, L	Lab	0*	Cr Life		
Saint Albans, D	Con	36	H		
St Aldwyn, E	Con	0	H	O	
St Davids, V	Con	66	H		
St Germans, E	Con	0	H	O	
St Helens, L		0	H		
St John of Bletso, L	XB	72	H		
St John of Fawsley, L	Con	70	Cr Life		
Saint Levan, L	Con	3	H		
Saint Oswald, L	Con	12	H		
St Vincent, V		0	H	O	A
Salisbury, M	Con	1	H	O	
Salisbury, Bp		0	Bp		
Saltoun of Abernethy, Ly	XB	53	H		

Title	Party	attendance	peerage type	oath	leave of absence
Samuel, V	XB	0	H		
Sandberg, L	LibDem	0*	Cr Life		
Sanderson of Bowden, L	Con	18	Cr Life		
Sandford, L	Con	19	H		
Sandhurst, L	XB	3	H		
Sandwich, E	XB	55	H		
Sandys, L	Con	18	H		
Savile, L	Con	27	H		
Saville of Newdigate, L	XB	0*	Cr Life		
Saye and Sele, L		0	H	O	A
Scanlon, L	Lab	14	Cr Life		
Scarbrough, E		0	H	O	
Scarman, L	XB	0	Cr App		
Scarsdale, V		0	H	O	
Scotland of Asthal, B	Lab	0*	Cr Life		
Seafield, E	Con	2	H		
Seccombe, B	Con	77	Cr Life		
Sefton of Garston, L	Lab	30	Cr Life		
Selborne, E	Con	40	H		
Selby, V		0	H	O	
Selkirk of Douglas, L	Con	0*	Cr Life		
Selsdon, L	Con	29	H		
Sempill, L	XB	18	H		
Serota, B	Lab	45	Cr Life		
Sewel, L	Lab	66	Cr Life		
Shaftesbury, E	Con	0	H	O	
Shannon, E	XB	78	H		
Sharples, B	Con	33	Cr Life		
Shaughnessy, L	XB	60	H		
Shaw of Northstead, L	Con	58	Cr Life		
Shawcross, L	XB	0	Cr Life	O	
Shepherd, L	Lab	45	H		
Sheppard of Didgemere, L	Con	7	Cr Life		
Sheppard of Liverpool, L		0*	Cr Life	O	
Sherfield, L		0	H	O	
Shore of Stepney, L	Lab	0*	Cr Life		
Shrewsbury, E	Con	38	H		
Shuttleworth, L	Con	9	H		
Sidmouth, V	XB	0	H		
Sieff of Brimpton, L	Con	0	Cr Life	O	
Silsoe, L		0	H	O	A
Simon, V	Lab	79	H		
Simon of Glaisdale, L	XB	77	Cr Life		
Simon of Highbury, L	Lab	0*	Cr Life		
Simon of Wythenshawe, L		0	H	O	
Simpson of Dunkeld, L	Lab	0*	Cr Life		
Sinclair, L		0	H	O	A
Sinclair of Cleeve, L		0	H	O	

Title	Party	attendance	peerage type	oath	leave of absence
Sinha, L		0	H	O	
Skelmersdale, L	Con	73	H		
Skidelsky, L	Con	43	Cr Life		
Sligo, M		0	H	O	
Slim, V	XB	49	H		
Slynn of Hadley, L	XB	20	Cr App		
Smith, L	XB	38	Cr Life		
Smith of Clifton, L	LibDem	0*	Cr Life		
Smith of Gilmorehill, B	Lab	57	Cr Life		
Snowdon, E	XB	0	Cr H	O	
Somerleyton, L	XB	2	H		
Somers, L		0	H	O	
Somerset, D	XB	5	H		
Soper, L	Lab	14	Cr Life		
Soulbury, V	XB	0	H	O	
Soulsby of Swaffham Prior, L	Con	61	Cr Life		
Southampton, L		0	H	O	
Southwell, Bp		9	Bp		
Spencer, E	XB	0	H	O	
Spens, L	XB	40	H		
Stafford, L	Con	10	H		
Stair, E	XB	0	H		
Stallard, L	Lab	77	Cr Life		
Stamp, L	XB	0	H		
Stanley of Alderley, L	Con	14	H		
Steel of Aikwood, L	LibDem	0*	Cr Life		
Sterling of Plaistow, L	Con	3	Cr Life		
Stevens of Ludgate, L	Con	7	Cr Life		
Stewartby, L	Con	68	Cr Life		
Steyn, L	XB	5	Cr App		
Stockton, E	Con	22	H		
Stodart of Leaston, L	Con	36	Cr Life		
Stoddart of Swindon, L	Lab	68	Cr Life		
Stokes, L	XB	1	Cr Life		
Stone of Blackheath, L	Lab	0*	Cr Life		
Strabolgi, L	Lab	77	H		
Stradbroke, E		0	H	O	
Strafford, E	XB	37	H		
Strang, L		0	H	O	
Strange, B	Con	60	H		
Strathalmond, L	XB	0	H		
Strathcarron, L	Con	63	H		
Strathclyde, L	Con	78	H		
Strathcona and Mount Royal, L	Con	41	H		
Stratheden and Campbell, L	XB	0	H	O	
Strathmore and Kinghorne, E	Con	7	H		
Strathspey, L		0	H	O	
Stuart of Findhorn, V		0	H	O	A
Sudeley, L	Con	62	H		

THE LORD NOLAN: *Of an appearance almost startling in its intelligence,* *Lord Nolan is a Law Lord, a staunch Catholic of Irish extraction* *and a very devoted family man*

THE LORD GOFF: *The Senior Law Lord, looking rather like a schoolmaster* *of sixty years ago, is a man of immense intellectual distinction. A former* *don at Oxford, he has written the standard work on the Law of Restitution*

Title	Party	attendance	peerage type	oath	leave of absence
Suffield, L	Con	5	H		
Suffolk and Berkshire, E	Con	15	H		
Sutherland, D		0	H	O	
Sutherland, C		0	H	O	
Swansea, L	XB	72	H		
Swaythling, L	Con	1	H		
Swinfen, L	Con	79	H		
Swinton, E	Con	18	H		
Symons of Vernham Dean, B	Lab	49*	Cr Life		
Sysonby, L		0	H	O	
Tankerville, E		0	H	O	
Tanlaw, L	XB	1	Cr Life		
Taverne, L	LibDem	69	Cr Life		
Taylor of Blackburn, L	Lab	75	Cr Life		
Taylor of Gryfe, L	Lab	55	Cr Life		
Taylor of Warwick, L	Con	61*	Cr Life		
Tebbit, L	Con	29	Cr Life		
Tedder, L		0	H	O	
Temple of Stowe, E	XB	13	H		
Templeman, L	XB	2	Cr App		
Tenby, V	XB	50	H		
Tennyson, L	XB	0	H	O	
Terrington, L	XB	75	H		
Teviot, L	Con	75	H		
Teynham, L	Con	68	H		
Thatcher, B	Con	5	Cr Life		
Thomas of Gresford, L	LibDem	59*	Cr Life		
Thomas of Gwydir, L	Con	73	Cr Life		
Thomas of Macclesfield, L	Lab	0*	Cr Life		
Thomas of Swynnerton, L	LibDem	10	Cr Life		
Thomas of Walliswood, B	LibDem	42	Cr Life		
Thomson of Fleet, L		0	H	O	
Thomson of Monifieth, L	LibDem	71	Cr Life		
Thurlow, L	XB	41	H		
Thurso, V	LibDem	43	H		
Tollemache, L	Con	16	H		
Tombs, L	XB	6	Cr Life		
Tope, L	LibDem	67	Cr Life		
Tordoff, L	LibDem	54	Cr Life		
Torphichen, L	Con	9	H		
Torrington, V	Con	17	H		
Townshend, M	Con	0	H	O	
Trefgarne, L	Con	46	H		
Trenchard, V	Con	1	H		
Trevethin and Oaksey, L	Con	1	H	O	
Trevor, L		0	H	O	
Trumpington, B	Con	75	Cr Life		

THE BARONESS JAMES OF HOLLAND PARK:
Better known as P.D. James,
she started writing her famous
thrillers shortly before the death
of her husband in 1964 in order
to help support her children.
She cares deeply
about the English language

THE LORD RATHCAVAN: *A former*
head of the Northern Irish Tourist
Board, Lord Rathcavan started
several highly successful
restaurants, and is now a walking
advertisement for the principle
of 'le patron mange ici'.
He has devoted much energy
to the promotion of Ulster food,
a cause which some would say
needs all the help it can get

Title	Party	attendance	peerage type	oath	leave of absence
Tryon, L	XB	2	H		
Tugendhat, L	Con	12	Cr Life		
Turner of Camden, B	Lab	73	Cr Life		
Tweeddale, M	XB	3	H		
Tweedsmuir, L	XB	8*	H		
Ullswater, V	Con	63	H		
Varley, L	Lab	23	Cr Life		
Vaux of Harrowden, L	Con	1	H	O	
Vernon, L		3	H	O	A
Verulam, E		0	H		
Vestey, L	Con	2	H		
Vincent of Coleshill, L	XB	1*	Cr Life		
Vinson, L	Con	19	Cr Life		
Vivian, L	Con	69	H		
Waddington, L	Con	0	Cr Life		
Wade of Chorlton, L	Con	49	Cr Life		
Wakefield, Bp		0*	Bp		
Wakeham, L	Con	52	Cr Life		
Wakehurst, L	Con	0	H		
Waldegrave, E	Con	0	H	O	
Wales, P	XB	0	Cr H	O	
Walker of Doncaster, L	Lab	0*	Cr Life		
Walker of Worcester, L	Con	21	Cr Life		
Wallace of Coslany, L	Lab	26	Cr Life		
Wallace of Saltaire, L	LibDem	47	Cr Life		
Walpole, L	XB	41	H		
Walsingham, L		0	H	O	
Walton of Detchant, L	XB	47	Cr Life		
Wardington, L	Con	0	H		
Warnock, B	XB	47	Cr Life		
Waterford, M	Con	11	H		
Watson of Invergowrie, L	Lab	0*	Cr Life		
Waverley, V	XB	77	H		
Weatherill, L	XB	79	Cr Life		
Wedderburn of Charlton, L	Lab	22	Cr Life		
Wedgwood, L	Con	10	H		
Weidenfeld, L	XB	8	Cr Life		
Weinstock, L	XB	3	Cr Life		
Weir, V	Con	1	H		
Wellington, D	XB	3	H		
Wemyss and March, E	Con	0	H		
Westbury, L	Con	74	H		
Westminster, D	Con	0	H	O	
Westmorland, E	XB	11	H		
Westwood, L		0	H	O	

THE LORD REAY: *His etiolated looks, air of langour and sartorial elegance do not suggest someone who has served on the front bench of the Conservative Government in the Lords. However, he was a government whip from 1989-91 and government spokesman for Environment, the Home Office and other departments from 1991-2. He would have made an excellent subject for Gainsborough*

THE EARL OF LONGFORD *From an Anglo-Irish Conservative family, Lord Longford is a Roman Catholic by adoption rather than by birth. He was given a hereditary peerage (Life peerages not yet existing) by the Labour Government in 1945, and became a Labour minister in the Lords. In 1961 he succeeded to the Longford title on the death of his elder brother. He is therefore in the unusual position of holding two hereditary peerages. Well-known for his interest in prison reform and convicted murderers, Lord Longford is a living argument for the hereditary system that he probably wants to abolish*

Title	Party	attendance	peerage type	oath	leave of absence
Whaddon, L	Lab	68	Cr Life		
Wharncliffe, E		0	H	O	
Wharton, B	XB	72	H		
White, B	Lab	64	Cr Life		
Whitelaw, V	Con	44	Cr H		
Whitty, L	Lab	53*	Cr Life		
Wigoder, L	LibDem	62	Cr Life		
Wigram, L	Con	8	H		
Wilberforce, L	XB	73	Cr App		
Wilcox, B	Con	63	Cr Life		
Williams of Crosby, B	LibDem	19	Cr Life		
Williams of Elvel, L	Lab	79	Cr Life		
Williams of Mostyn, L	Lab	65	Cr Life		
Willoughby de Broke, L	Con	24	H		
Willoughby de Eresby, B	XB	11	H		
Wilson, L		0	H	O	
Wilson of Tillyorn, L	XB	20	Cr Life		
Wilton, E		0	H		
Wimborne, V	XB	2*	H	O	
Winchester, M		0	H	O	
Winchester, Bp		8	Bp		
Winchilsea and Nottingham, E	LibDem	53	H		
Windlesham, L	Con	4	H		
Winston, L	Lab	55	Cr Life		
Wise, L	Con	77	H		
Wolfson, L	Con	10	Cr Life		
Wolfson of Sunningdale, L	Con	0	Cr Life		
Wolverton, L	XB	0	H	O	
Woolf, L	XB	8	Cr App		
Woolton, E	Con	11	H		
Wraxall, L		0	H	O	
Wrenbury, L	XB	10	H		
Wright of Richmond, L	XB	55	Cr Life		
Wrottesley, L	Con	10	H		
Wyfold, L		0	H	O	A
Wynford, L	Con	51	H		
Yarborough, E	Con	3	H		
York, D	XB	0	Cr H	O	
York, Abp		5	Bp		
Young, B	Con	64	Cr Life		
Young of Dartington, L	Lab	10	Cr Life		
Young of Graffham, L	Con	3	Cr Life		
Young of Old Scone, B	Lab	0*	Cr Life		
Younger of Leckie, V	Con	3	H		
Zetland, M	Con	0	H		
Zouche of Haryngworth, L	Con	14	H		

iv. COMPOSITION OF THE HOUSE OF LORDS BY PEERAGE TYPE

Archbishops and bishop	26
Peers by succession	750 (16 women)
Hereditary peers of first creation	9
Life peers under the Appellate Jurisdiction Act 1876	26
Life peers under the Life Peerages Act 1958	462 (80 women)
Total	**1,273**

of whom:

Lords without Writs of Summons	68 (2 minors)
Peers on leave of absence from the House	61

10 persons who had inherited peerages have disclaimed them for life
(3 of these now sit in the House by virtue of other titles).

v. COMPOSITION OF THE HOUSE OF LORDS BY RANK

Prince (of the Blood Royal)	1
Archbishops	2
Dukes + Dukes of Blood Royal	25+3
Marquesses	34
Earls + Countesses	169+5
Viscounts	103
Bishops	24
Barons + Baronesses + Ladies	816+88+3
Total	**1,273**

vi. PARTY STRENGTHS IN THE HOUSE OF LORDS

Party	Life Peers	Hereditary Peers of first creation	by succession	Lords Spiritual	Total
Conservative	172	4	319		495
Labour	140	1	16		157
Liberal Democrat	44	0	24		68
cross-bench	118	4	200		322
other	8	0	71	25	104
Total	482	9	630	25	1146

House of Lords Information Office, House of Lords, London SW1A 0PW
Telephone: 0171 219 3107
http://www.parliament.uk
© Parliamentary copyright House of Lords

vii. LIFE PEERAGES ANNOUNCED ON 20 JUNE 1998

Baronesses

Peta Jane Buscombe

Christine Mary Crawley

Mary Teresa Goudie

Sue Miller

Margaret Lucy Sharp

Glenys Thornton

Polla Manzila Uddin

Barons

Nazir Ahmed

Waheed Alli

William Stephen Goulden Bach

Sir Timothy John Leigh Bell

Melvyn Bragg

David Keith Brookman

Anthony Martin Grosvenor Christopher C.B.E.

Anthony James Clarke C.B.E.

David Evans

Jonathan Toby Harris

Christopher Robin Haskins

Timothy Francis Clement-Jones C.B.E.

The Right Honourable Norman Stewart Hughson Lamont

Brian Mackenzie O.B.E.

Professor Philip Norton

Andrew Wyndham Phillips O.B.E.

Thomas Sawyer

John Edward Tomlinson

Norman Warner

Paul Edward Winston White

PICTURE CREDITS

HarperCollins*Publishers* would like to thank the following for their kind permission to reproduce the photographs in this book:

Hulton Getty Images Limited 141 (bottom), 146

Mary Evans Picture Library 70,

Popperfoto 89

Reproduced by kind permission of the Palace of Westminster 24, 69, 73, 87, 139 (bottom), 140, 141

Tate Gallery, London 1998 71

The British Architectural Library, RIBA, London 76, 77

The Country Life Picture Library 84, 135, 139 (top), 141

The Illustrated London News Picture Library 80,

V&A Picture Library endpapers, 78

All other photographs supplied by **Derry Moore**.

Index

Page references in *italics* refer to illustrations of individuals